SONGS OF THE BARDS O

Nabanidās Bāul with his *aektārā*

SONGS OF THE BARDS OF BENGAL

TRANSLATED FROM THE ORIGINAL BENGALI
WITH INTRODUCTION AND NOTES
BY
DEBEN BHATTACHARYA

GROVE PRESS, INC., NEW YORK

First published as *The Mirror of the Sky*, by George Allen & Unwin Ltd., London, 1969

UNESCO COLLECTION OF REPRESENTATIVE WORKS INDIAN SERIES. This book has been accepted in the Indian Series of the Translations Collection of the United Nations Educational, Scientific and Cultural Organization (UNESCO).

Library of Congress Catalog Number: 72-110 333

First Evergreen Edition 1969

First Printing

Manufactured in the United States of America

The Mirror of the Sky

The mirror of the sky
Reflects my soul.
O Bāul of the road,
O Bāul, my heart,
What keeps you tied
To the corner of a room?

As the storm rampages
In your crumbling hut,
The water rises to your bed.
Your torn-apart quilt
Is afloat on the flood,
Leaving your shelter down.

O Bāul of the road,
O Bāul, my heart,
What keeps you tied
To the corner of a room?

Anon[1]

[1] Tape-recorded in Varanasi, in 1954.

ACKNOWLEDGMENTS

I am deeply indebted to Cristopher Nash for generous guidance during my revising the manuscript and for offering many valuable suggestions. I must also express my gratitude to Richard Lannoy who supplied me with the photographs reproduced in this book.

FOREWORD

The word *bāul* appears for the first time in literature in the Bengali poetic works of the fifteenth and sixteenth centuries, *Shri Krishna-vijaya* by Maladhar Basu and *Chaitanya-charitāmrita* by Krishnadas Kaviraj. It is generally agreed that the word *bāul* in Bengali is a derivation of Sanskrit *vātul*, meaning mad, affected by wind.

Modern literary interest in the works of the Bāuls was roused in 1925 by Rabindranath Tagore. He first lectured on them at Calcutta University, and later in Oxford, and is considered one of the pioneers among the collectors of Bāul songs. Shri Kshitimohan Sen Shastri, a colleague of the poet in Viswa-Bharati University, is another pioneer; and amongst the later collectors, Professor Upendranath Bhattacharya has fulfilled a gigantic task by publishing a selection of over five hundred songs from his vast collection, together with notes, commentaries and background history.

The song of the Bāuls were not written for the reading public, neither were they intended as literary or artistic works. As a matter of fact, in the past most of the Bāuls were unable to read or write and this is still the case today.

The texts were created for oral transmission with the aid of music, for religious reasons. The purpose of the songs was to impart teaching from master to disciple.

The poetic merit of the text is purely incidental, produced by the depth of the Bāul's feelings and his ability to give sound to them in simple village language. There is no trace of conscious 'poetic' calculation in the songs of the Bāuls.

The two most important sources of the texts available are collections made by the Bāuls themselves, and a Bāul poet who is still living today. Unfortunately neither is one hundred per cent reliable. The collections, written down by semi-literate hands, are not always recorded faithfully, and the poet has the habit of leaving his own mark on the songs, either deliberately or because of an occasional lapse of memory. It is therefore almost certain that the songs given here will differ from the originals.

The translator's task, in this particular case, is made doubly difficult by the added responsibility of having to translate words of orally transmitted songs, into an alien language.

A number of the songs, in their original versions, are concerned with the more complicated aspects of the Bāul's religious tradition. None of these can be reproduced in word-for-word translation without elaborate explanatory notes. I have included only a few examples of these, mainly concentrating on those which deal with the philosophy of the Bāuls and which can bear the strain of translation.

Although I feel that poetry, either in its original language or in translation, ought to be readable without the help of pedantic explanations, in the interest of meaning I have sometimes had to content myself with the presentation of fragments or with the addition of a brief commentary on what might otherwise seem too obscure.

In addition to my own tape-recordings of the Bāul songs collected during years of field work in India, in my selection for this volume I have consulted *Bānglār Bāul* by Kshitimohan Sen Shastri, Calcutta, 1954; *Lālan Gītikā*, edited by Dr Matilal Das and Shri Piyushkanti Mahapatra, Calcutta, 1958; *Bānglār Palligīti* by Chittaranjan Deva, Calcutta, 1966; *Bānglār Bāul—Kāvya O Darshan* by Shri Somendranath Bandopadhyay, Calcutta, 1964; *Bānglār Sādhak Bāul* by Shrimati Indira Devi, Calcutta, 1962; and *Bānglār Bāul O Bāul Gān* by Professor Upendranath Bhattacharya,[1] Calcutta, 1957.

According to the poetic tradition of Bengal, in particular that of the Vaishnava poetry (*see note* on p. 27), some well-known Bāuls have inserted their names in the last verses of their songs, making identification possible. On the other hand, a large number of songs which are still sung, or those which have been collected from copyists' notebooks, have no such signature lines. These songs are grouped in the section entitled 'anonymous'.

The biographical history of the individual Bāul, too, if often based entirely on word-of-mouth, and therefore is not always available. Factual information such as dates of birth and death,

[1] For this and much other material concerning the Bāul, I am deeply indebted to Professor Upendranath Bhattacharya.

the name of the village where the Bāul was born and where he lived, in a number of cases cannot be obtained. The biographical notes toward the end of the book, therefore, refer only to those on whom we have information accepted by specialists.

The songs of the Bāuls explore the worlds of the invisible and the unattainable; they are not merely conventionally organized expressions of feelings illustrated by poetic images. Although some of the songs are a little too long-winded, this large selection is representative of Bāul art and shows the true creative intuition of these people.

DEBEN BHATTACHARYA

CONTENTS

FOREWORD *page* 11

INTRODUCTION 23

Outline of the Historical Background 25

Songs of the Bāuls 26

The Bāul Faith 31

THE SONGS

Each of us 39
Scanning the cosmos 39
Attested by your own heart 40
Whom will you regard 40
The ways of the tortuous river 40
Only a connoisseur 41
Mad, mad 42
According to the views of the world 42
The rites of spring 43
Nothing has happened 43
Come if you wish to meet 44
Commit yourself to the earth 45
Raise the torch of love 45
The potter 46
O my senseless heart 46
You must be singleminded 47
How could he stand 47
What dealings 48
He is watching the path 48
Dear love 49
What colour is your cottage 50
If you wish to board an aeroplane 50
That astounding engine 51
O, my heart 51

Who gave shape 52
The heart, a lotus 53
The essence of love 54
Each fruit is open to 54
Human limbs 54
Let ripeness appear 55
The milk of the lioness 55
The master of the universe 56
My worries continue 56
My unknowing heart 57
Never plunge 57
Go to the home 57
To find nectar 58
My soul cries out 58
My life is a little oil lamp 58
The eyes see 59
What is the use 60
I often repeat 60
That enchanting river 61
The leaves are bejewelled 61
God has reversed the acts 62
Sown on a slab of stone 62
Forget not 63
When the confluence 63
The man that breathes 64
Reaching for reality 65
Where is the home 65
The rites of ferocious love 66
I am forbidden to reveal 67
Will the day ever dawn 67
Those who are dead 68
Free impulses 68
He who knows 69
How can you walk 69
When the life 70
On the other shore 70
Release the sensation 71
Light has burst 71

My lord is not a broken wheel 72
My heart is saturated 72
I am fulfilled 72
How can I capture the man 73
Blind one 73
Pour out 74
Look, look for him 74
I plunged into the water 75
Tribeni 75
Ploughman 76
Shame to you 77
If you fail to recognize 77
The body of man 78
The primeval man 78
Gay and glorious 79
Let your heart be a caring home 79
Poison that kills the man 79
Formless 80
And as yet 80
Never in my life 81
No words can describe the chātaka 81
I have no knowledge 82
Can I ever again be born 83
My heart is not 84
I wish to go to Kāshi 84
This land offered me 84
How long shall it be 84
My heart 85
Please, Kānāi 85
What is the colour of your love 86
Poison and nectar 86
Who is there for you 87
A man unknown to me 87
He talks to me 88
As the man and the women in me 88
The moon is encircled by moons 89
Pandemonium broke loose 89
The key to my own home 90

Could I ever forget him 90
Sixteen gangsters 91
I am afraid 91
How the days drag 92
The road to you is blocked 93
Even if you forbid 93
O cruelly eager 93
The subterranean stream 94
I shall not open my eyes again 94
The so-called lovers 95
Your heart 95
The act of loving 96
Groping for the river 96
Plunging deep into the sea 97
Cry for the unknown 97
I wished to turn myself 98
From the distance of millions of miles 98
The moon rises 98
My eyes are drowned by shadows 99
Do you wish to visit my 99
Not one single branch 100
Will the man of love 100
O my heart 101
In vain do you worry 101
The secret of feeling 102
What makes you think 102
Brothers 103
How can the rays of the sun 103
Strike your master hard 103
The shapes you have formed 104
With a beggar's humility 104
What good is there 105
That astounding flower 105
He who has seen the beauty 105
He who knows the ways 106
You may hurt me, my lord 107
Ants wishing to fly 107
A leper does not worry 107

The act of finding 107
A restless rutting elephant repels control 108
Have you tallied 108
O my heart 109
While desire 109
Explore the nature 110
The man is living in man 110
Now is the time for you 111
My heart is eager enough 111
My plaited hair 112
My heart 112
A creature of lust 113

NOTES ON THE POETS 114

BIBLIOGRAPHY 117

DISCOGRAPHY 118

INDEX 119

ILLUSTRATIONS

1	Nabanidās Bāul with his *aektārā*	*frontispiece*
2	Nabanidās Bāul	32
3	*Ānandalahari*	48
4	Purna Chandra Bāul (with *ānandalahari* and	64
	Sudhā Bāul (with the lute *dotārā*)	80
5	Bāul instruments	
6	Nabanidās Bāul, in meditation	80

INTRODUCTION

The name 'Bāul' has been given to a small collection of individuals with a distinctive religious belief, from the village labouring classes of Bengal. To the average Bengali, the Bāul is unconventional to the point of being bizarre, but he demands love and respect for his songs.

According to the Bāul's description of himself, he is '. . . wholly dedicated to his own nature. He laughs or cries, dances or begs as he wishes. . . . He lives a strange life, almost insane, with values of his own but contrary to others. His home being under the tree, he moves from district to district, all the year round, as a dancing beggar who owns nothing in the world but a ragged patchwork quilt.'[1]

Even today, in spite of the problems of partition and poverty, folk songs and dances and village poetry of socio-religious origin are still very important to the Bengalis. They have many varieties of folk art, for example, *gambhirā* and *gājan* dances, *jhāpān* and *karam* songs, *pāñchāli* and *bratakathā* poems, and all of these have some sort of religious associations. Both men and women participate in the singing, in cities as well as in villages, once or more, depending on the occasion, with every full moon. An expectant mother will visit the village banyan tree that shelters the clay figure of the goddess *Shashthi* to recite her verses of praise to the goddess in shy whispers, praying for the well-being and stout health of her child. On Saturday evenings men will intone, either singly or in a group, the rhymed lines of a long balladlike text which describes the exploits of Shani, the Saturn, the astral god that rules the day of the week.

The Bāul can be described as a cultural and religious nomad among the peasant *bourgeoisie* of Bengal. He uses the peasant language and imagery, and he lives with the peasant. Yet he is not a peasant. He is not attached to the land. His songs speak against attachment, even to people who adore their '*golden Bānglā*' lying between the great Kanchan-janghā peaks in the north and the Bay of Bengal in the south.

[1] Anonymous.

Immense rivers, descending from the Himalayas, and merging into the ocean, weave a network of arteries across Bengal. The climate is tamed and temperate for most of the year, but during the summer monsoon when the humid warm air from the ocean hits the mountain walls, it bursts into sudden explosions of lightning and thunder, storms and rains. The rivers swell up to destroy and to bring a renewed life to the land. While villages and habitations are wiped out by inundation, forests grow thicker. Jute stems shoot up resisting the decaying power of the water and the rice fields turn golden with the ripening of the paddy corns at the end of the monsoon.

Fishermen, who have been risking their lives, set their sails on the calm rivers again as lines of coconut palms and the plantain foliage screen the village. Lotuses return to the village pond and the fragrance of the *champak* flower fills the land.

Folk festivities continue throughout the year, at every season, even during the height of the monsoon, and most are concerned with the river. The Bengalis have learned to live with the knowledge that the river's power is twofold: it is the bringer of destruction and of fertility, of death and of life. Images of it recur in the Bāul songs:

> Never plunge
> into the river of lust,
> you will not reach the shores.
> It is a river of no coasts
> where typhoons rage . . . .[1]

There are also songs in its praise:

> That enchanting river
> reflects the very form
> of the formless one.
> Sense the essence of the matter. . . .[2]

The Bāul is undeniably a product of the Bengali village. His basic personality is deeply rooted in the land from which he seeks freedom; his philosophy is the conscious enquiry of a simple peasant mind. In his search for God he brings the physical world to his aid:

[1] By Dwija Kailāshchandra.

[2] By Gopāl.

The body of man
is a land for wish-fulfilling—
care will produce
a harvest of jewels.
Plough it in a propitious time.
Hopes that ushered you
to this material world
will bear fruit. . . .[1]

Outline of the Historical Background

Because Bengal never wholly identified itself with the history of the Aryans as did the rest of north India, its history is almost impossible to separate from ancient folklore. This is also true of the history of the Bāul. The Sanskrit-speaking invaders from the north had stopped abruptly at the border of Bengal and remained there for several centuries, viewing the country with suspicion from the neighbouring outposts. It was their first encounter with the northern tropics, and they announced that the east was occupied by huntsmen with strange habits. It was advisable to call a halt to further advance to the east.

We have no definite information about the nature of early Jain and Buddhist contacts with Bengal. Even if these cultures did leave an impression, it was so negligible as to have little bearing on later history.

It was not until the fourth century AD, when Bengal came under the political domination of the Gupta Empire, that the intellectual influence of the Sanskrit made itself felt. The Aryanized history of Bengal begins at this period, for it is then, either as an independent power, or politically controlled, that Bengal becomes closely connected with the rest of Sanskrit-speaking India.

The Gupta rule lasted for over two centuries in Bengal. While the ruling classes and the intellectuals became thoroughly involved with Vedic Hindu thought which was rapidly absorbing many non-Aryan elements from the land, the folk religions were given a cloak of Sanskrit respectability. The sturdy fertility goddess of the countryside, the notoriously self-opinionated Saturn, and many other village gods and goddesses were now

[1] By Kālāchānd.

endowed with a few verses of praise in Sanskrit in addition to the existing peasant ballads.

After the Gupta period most of Bengal continued to be ruled by Hindu kings until the middle of the eighth century, when the country came under the powerful Buddhist Pāla kings. The majority of the population, particularly those who were socially humble, adopted the rulers' religion and Bengal became one of the most important grounds for the dissemination of the Buddhist ideals. The Pālas ruled till the middle of the twelfth century when they were replaced by the Senas, the Vaishnava Hindus from the south, whose reign lasted for a little over a hundred years.

Toward the close of the thirteenth century, the whole of Bengal was in Muslim hands; fanatic efforts were made to proselytize the Hindus and the Buddhists into Islam. This had an important bearing in the development of the Bāul tradition. A large number of Muslims, presumably some of those who were converted during the Islamic expansion in Bengal, and a certain section of the Sūfīs, the mystics of Islam, took to the Bāul faith.

The Muslim domination of Bengal ended with the British entry, and the history of British India has no direct relationship to the history of the Bāuls.

Songs of the Bāuls

The oldest of the Bāul songs available today were composed during the eighteenth century; but they were not written down, either because the Bāul was incapable of doing so or because he did not have any urge to make his creation permanent. As he did not believe in propaganda or conversion, he made his songs for himself and for his disciples' instruction—they were his way of coming to terms with God and love, life and death, society and the individual.

The songs do not show any trace of collective thinking, neither is there any suggestion of preaching. They are composed by individuals, in simple village language, using regional vocabulary and sung in the intonation of the district of their origin. The images are mostly of village scenes, objects used in the everyday life of the inhabitants, and caricatures of the different professions within the Bāul community. The songs might be grouped under the following headings:

(*a*) Appeals to the teacher and the enquiries into the nature of God.

(*b*) Spiritual union with God: 'the man of the heart', 'the unattainable man'.

(*c*) Metaphysical analysis of the human body and the material world.

(*d*) Physical and mental disciplines for spiritual development.

(*e*) Questions regarding life and death and the understanding of death coupled with the striving to be fully alive.

(*f*) Futility of doctrinaire social and religious systems and the traditions of caste, class and race.

From the point of view of formal poetry the Bāuls have little to offer of aesthetic merit. Their vocabulary is colloquial and limited, and the rhythmic structures of the verses often slack, monotonous and impetuous. Obviously, the words of the songs have been put together not for the rhythm of the poetry but with the melody of the song in mind, with the result that a syllable here and there has been prolonged or shortened according to the need of the melody. Following the tradition of Bengali poetry of the period, the verses are usually rhymed.

The meters employed by the Bāul spring mainly from village poetry and the Vaishnava poems,[1] but as can be seen from the following example, the Bāul leaves his own mark on the meter This meter, entitled *dhāmāli*, is fairly popular with the Vaishnava poets. It is even in its metric structure and the time-division of each line is 4 4 4 2. The quotation below, from a song by the Bāul, Bishā Bhuñimālī, shows how flexible is the Bāul's approach to the accepted metrical form. While he maintains the set time-division in the first half of the stanza, in the second half he takes advantage of the Bāul's usual privilege—the freedom of action:

chhédé jété lobhi bhramar

4 4

[1] See *Love Songs of Chandidās*, Deben Bhattacharya, London, 1967. Chandidās is considered the father of the Bengali Vaishnava poetry on the theme of Rādhā and Krishna's romance. This theme, as a subject for poetry, became extremely popular in Bengal following the Vaishnava religious movement which was sparked off by Shri Chaitanya Deva during the sixteenth century.

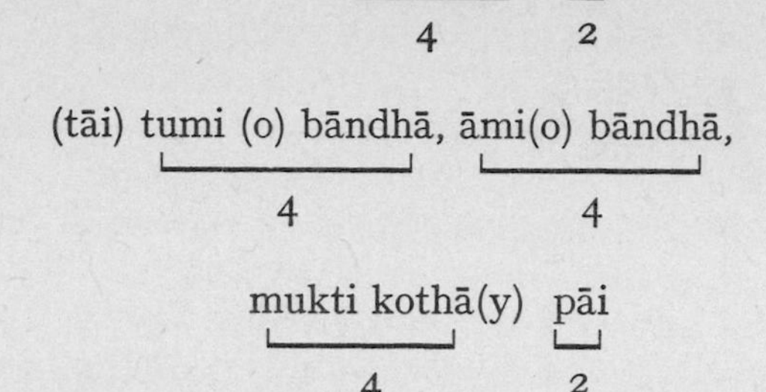

The extra syllables used by the Bāul Bishā Bhuñimālī are in parentheses. The words of the quotation mean:

> The bee is avid
> And unable to leave.
> So, you are bound
> And I am bound—
> Where is freedom then?

Generally speaking, the songs are sung to the accompaniment of instrumental music, the instruments being:

(1) The *gopijantra* or the *aektārā*. It is a one-stringed drone instrument. The string is plucked by a wire plectrum fitted to the index finger. The belly of the instrument is made of an open-headed calabash and the neck is a meter-long bamboo which is split down the middle. The two halves of the split bamboo neck are then fixed symmetrically to the open end of the gourd.

(2) The next in importance is the *ānandalahari*, or the *gubgubi*, or the *khamak*. This is a plucking drum with a pair of gut strings attached to the skin of a foot-long, one-headed drum. The other ends of the gut strings are fixed to a small drum, no bigger than a coffee cup. This small drum, held in the left hand of the drummer, keeps the gut strings taut, while the big drum, hanging from his left shoulder, is kept tightly pressed under his arm. By tightening and relaxing the gut strings, as he strikes them with a plectrum, the Bāul controls the variation of the pitch.

(3) *Dotārā*. This is a four-stringed long-necked lute. The

belly of the instrument is covered by goat skin. The lute is played with a plectrum. This instrument is extremely popular in different types of folk music all over Bengal.

(4) The *duggi* is a kettle drum which is tied to the Bāul's waist. As he dances, he plays it with one hand and accompanies himself on the drone instrument, *gopijantra,* with the other.

(5) The *juri* is a pair of small bell-metal cymbals.

Poetry, music, song and dance are all essential to the Bāul, and all are devoted to one main end. This is the search to find man's relationship with God, and to discover the purpose of man's existence:

> O my senseless heart,
> you have failed to cultivate
> the humanland . . . ,
> Cultivated,
> it could have yielded a harvest of gold. . . .[1]

Most of the Bāul songs are based on the enquiry into oneself and one's relationship with God. As we are discussing the subject elsewhere in detail, we shall concentrate here mainly on the technical and social aspects of the Bāul songs.

The Bāul earns most of his living from his songs, which he sings travelling from door to door. The donations are considered a form of charity in Bengal, but the position of the collector is one of dignity. When singing alone in front of a village audience, the Bāul sings, dances, and plays the string drone *gopijantra* and the kettle-drum, *duggi,* and singing in a group, he may use more than two instruments, depending on the availability of players. Clusters of small bells tied round his ankles give the rhythm of his dance. The melodies of his songs are often a blending of two or more tunes. They are rooted in the regional folk music of Bengal, but have a distinctive form and a style of their own, a style so individual that it has come to be known as the *Bāulsur,* the melody of the Bāul.

The Bāul's voice is not always melodious or pleasant to listen to. During my recording of Nabanidās Bāul[2] in Siuri, a small village in Birbhum, Nabanidās had lost his voice owing

[1] Anonymous.
[2] Songs sung by Nabanidās Bāul are reproduced on pp. 47, 102 and 112.

to an overdose of the hemp he had been smoking before he started singing. The small crowd gathered in the sweet shop, listening to him, did not care about the quality of his voice for he was able to communicate to them naturally, effortlessly. Through his songs, Nabanidās directed his questions and answers to himself, and yet he was able to stir every single individual in this random gathering. The audience sat listening, spellbound, and asked him to sing over and over again. One of his songs started with this challenge:

What makes you think
You are human?
Having squandered
Your heritage of heart,
You are now lost in lust . . .[1]

Neither the singer nor the audience could be described as sophisticated, but no one took any notice of the tape-recorder. The listeners were wholly absorbed by the theme of the song, with every word of it. An Indian audience is usually critical of the timbre or the quality of the voice, but when it comes to songs of introspective nature, they can become easily involved with the spirit of the text. If the singer has a cold or some other malady which makes his voice hoarse, the audience is understanding; but if his art is bad, they can be as unkind as any Western audience.

The Bāul tradition spread all over Bengal. More than forty famous Bāuls and a large number of anonymous songwriters emerged since the beginning of the eighteenth century.

Socially, the Bāul tradition can be interpreted as a series of rebellions by isolated individualists against caste and class systems. It started as a revolt against the conventions of the established religions, Islam and the Hindu faith, and it has remained involved with both. Less frequently, the songs have attacked social inequality:

The rites of spring
Have burst in the Tāj Mahal . . .
Little sons of pigs
Who are ruled by the powerful king,

[1] By Padmalochan.

Have taken charge of all.
The rites of spring
Have burst in the Tāj Mahal . . .[1]

There can be nothing more revolutionary than the idea of holding a spring festival in the Tāj Mahal, the very seat of Islamic imperial power. The *dol,* the colour festival of the springtime, is essentially Hindu and is alien to the orthodox Islam.

For a simple rural people with very little or no literary training, the Bāul have a unique sensibility. Just as they will accept nothing which is offered ready-made, they discard nothing that can be translated into the Bāul language. Here is a Bāul song with a modern subject and images of the mechanized world, but composed in the Bāul idiom:

If you wish to board an aeroplane,
you must travel light
to be safe from the danger of a crash.
You must renounce
your errors and inhibitions . . .[2]

The Bāul faith

The most distinctive quality of Bāul religious thought is its robust simplicity and directness of expression:

When the life,
The mind
And the eyes
Are in agreement,
The target is
Within your reach:
You can see
The formless *Brahma*
With bare eyes . . .[3]

The Bāul accepts that God is formless, but to him form and the formless are one and inseparable; what matters most

[1] Anonymous. See *Bengal*—Phillips Phonographic Industries, Baarn, Holland, record No. 427 016 NE, series *Song and Sound.*
[2] Anonymous.
[3] By Hāude Gosāiñ.

to the Bāul is the interrelationship between God and existence, the universe:

. . . Forget not
that your body contains
the whole of existence.[1]

In his attitude to God and the universe, the Bāul is closer to the religious thought of the *Tantras* than that of the Vedas. The *Vedas* were brought by the Aryans, and in general deal with the gods related to nature, such as those of the sun and the rains, and place value on masculinity as personified by tough animal-breeders. The *Tantras*, on the other hand, reflect the ancient folklore of the land of pre-Aryan times; though much of it has been discreetly aryanized. It deals with the domain of the mind, the known and the unknown spheres of human psychology, and masculine power and female energy both in sex and in the search for God. In the *Tantras* the worlds of God, demon, and man, the abstract and the tangible, are all the reflections of the same vital force:

'All physical and mental forms, everything in the universe, is that one, appearing in various ways. Life is one, all its forms are interrelated in a vastly complicated but inseparable whole. Every act by any form of life, from the highest to the lowest, must react on every other form. We are but links in a long series. We are made of the same substance as the stars, the same substance as the gods.'[2]

There is, however, one respect in which the Bāul and the *Tantra* differ in their attitude to love. The approach of the *Tantras* is earthy and harsh. They take the impulses and passions into account only in order to be free of them. They have little patience for the emotional sublimation of the impulses, such as love, which does not strike the *Tantra* mind as reliable, whereas to the Bāul, love is nearly a synonym for God:

Lust and love
and the erotic acts
are housed in one single place. . . .[3]

[1] By Gosāiñ Gopāl.
[2] *Tantra Art*, Ajit Mukerjee, Kumar Gallery, Paris—New Delhi, 1966.
[3] By Hāude Gosāiñ.

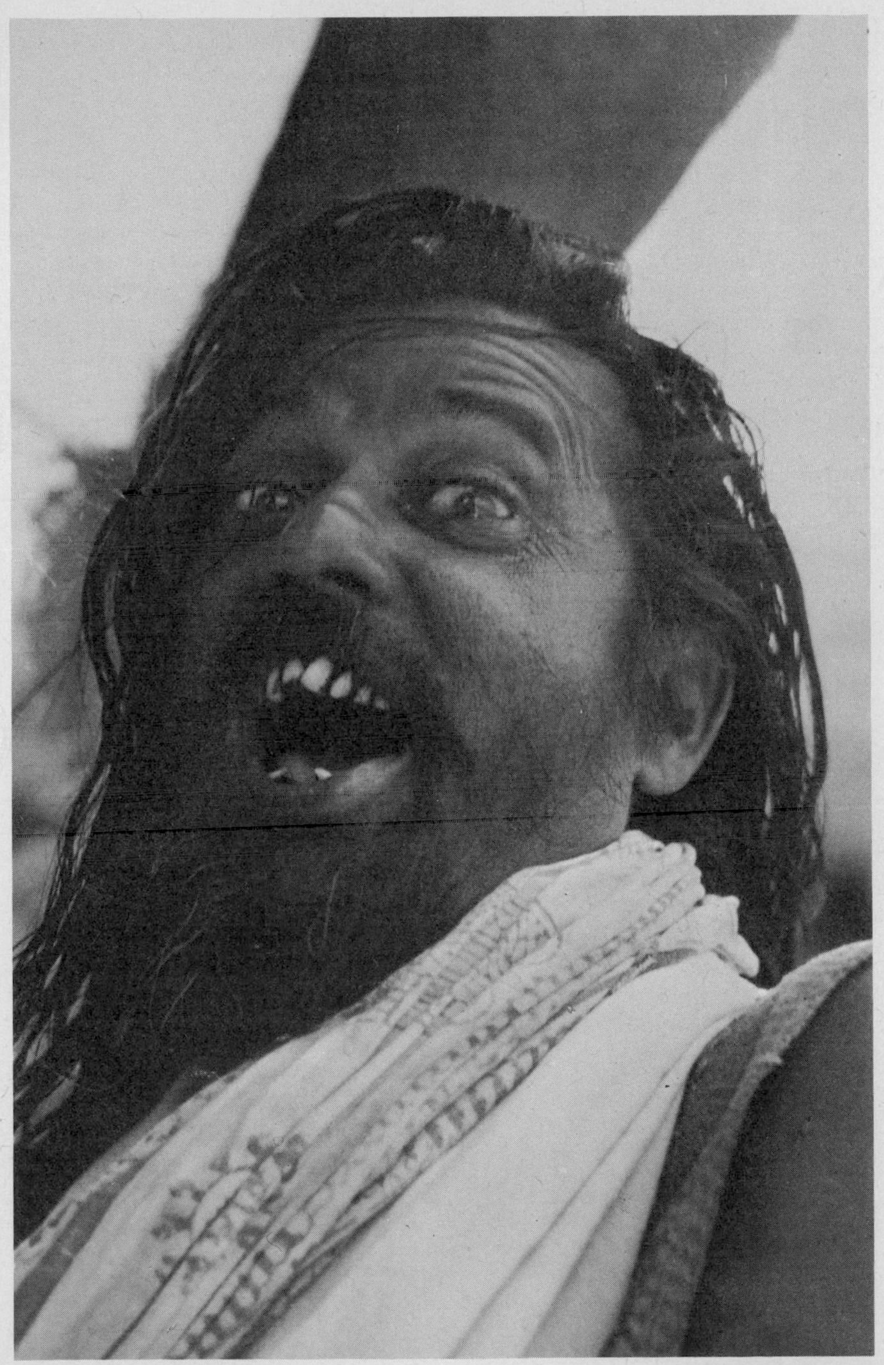

Nabanidās Bāul 2

Owing to his lack of conventional leanings, the Bāul is able to surpass most others in directness of expression:

The essence of love
lies in carnal lust
Bearing a deep secret.
Only lovers
can unravel it. . . .[1]

This emphasis on love in Bāul literature suggests the influence of the Vaishnava religious tradition which overran Bengal during the leadership of Shri Chaitanya Deva AD 1486–1533. According to Shri Chaitanya, God is indivisible. There is no separation between the creator and the created. A devotee must utilize the compulsive power of his own emotion in trying to find union with God. And in loving God, he must be free from any motive other than the desire to love. But Shri Chaitanya did not take the physical impulses of love into account, whereas the *Tantra* did. And so did the Bāul.

The Bāul combined Shri Chaitanya's path of devotion with the realism of the *Tantras*. He was able to say with conviction:

Release the sensation
of taste
on your tongue.
Open the doors of feeling . . .
Lust and love
and the erotic acts
are housed in one single place
where sorrows and joys
do not exist. . . .[2]

At the same time, the Bāul could find himself sharing Shri Chaitanya's devotion and express himself with the lyricism of the Vaishnava poetry:[3]

I am fulfilled
Being a blow of your own breath—
On your flute . . .

[1] By Chandidās Gosāiñ.
[2] By Hāude Gosāiñ.
[3] See note on Vaishnava poetry, p. 27.

What more can I wish for me
Than to be blown away with such melody.[1]

It is not only possible to compare Bāul thought with a number of existing philosophies in India, it has also much in common with Sūfī mysticism. Indeed, a poem quoted below by the Persian Sūfī poet Jalalu'l-Din Rumi bears a striking resemblance, in both its poetic form and in the intensity of its devotion, to the above-quoted Bāul song.

We have already mentioned that the Bāuls come from both the Hindu and the Muslim communities in Bengal. It is quite usual for a Muslim Bāul to have a Hindu teacher or for a Hindu Bāul to sing Islamic songs. To the Bāul, the conventions of Islam and Hinduism are equally meaningless, but to break away from the established institutions in order to set up new ones would demand too much of them. They therefore choose to remain in the no-man's-land between the two.

Poetic mysticism is found in nearly all religions, both in the East and in the West. In the *Mathnawi*, Jalalu'l-Din Rumi (AD 1207–1273), describes the soul's liberation from self while it is filled with the love of God:

. . . 'Tis the flame of Love that fired me
'Tis the wine of Love inspired me.
Wouldst though learn how lovers bleed,
Hearken, hearken to the Reed! [2]

Similarly, St John of the Cross in his 'Songs of the Soul in Rapture' worships God with the devotion of a lover:

. . . Within my flowering breast
Which only for himself entire I save
He sank into his rest
And all my gifts I gave
Lulled by the airs with which the cedars wave. [3]

The *Rig Veda*, the earliest sacred text of India, compiled in approximately 1500 BC, talks to God with friendly intimacy:

[1] By Ishān Jugi.
[2] *RUMI—Poet and Mystic*, Reynold A. Nicholson, London, 1956.
[3] *St John of the Cross*, translated by Roy Campbell, London, 1960.

In your boat, my lord,
you and I, the two close friends,
were afloat on the sea.
Why do you wish to destroy me now?
Where has our friendship gone?[1]

But the Bāul has a sturdier approach to the Almighty. Firmly believing that God is housed within himself, he finds that there is little use in projecting his complaints outward. Instead, he challenges God:

You may hurt me, my lord,
go, hurt me
as long as I can bear the pain.[2]

Some scholars have attempted to associate Bāul belief with Vedic thought,[3] but the arguments in favour of this association are not convincing. The *Vedas* were occupied with establishing Hindu religious rites and the sanctity of the Brahmanic hierarchy against which the Bāuls, like the Buddhists, rebelled. Though most Indian thought derives something from vast Vedic literature, centuries old, Vedic poetry was far too abstract and dry to have inspired the Bāuls, whose songs spring from the heart. For example, in discussing the relationship between life and death, the *Rig Veda* says:

Life lives on the dead,
Life and death spring from the same source.[4]

Life and death are also prominent in Bāul poetry, but the approach to the problem is completely different from that of the herdsmen who had to live on the food their cattle provided. The Bāul's interpretation of the question is less didactic and severe. His enquiry, instead of emphasizing the means by which one lived, treats God, the 'man of the heart', as the focal point:

. . . The man you seek
is earthed
in the earth,

[1] *Rig Veda* 7. 88. 3–5.
[2] By Podu.
[3] *Bānglār Bāul*, Kshitimohan Sen Shastri, Calcutta, 1954.
[4] *Rig Veda* 1. 164. 30.

deceased while being.
Dying with death,
you must live to seek . . .[1]

The Vedic statement is connected with the tangible, that which can be rationally explained. The Bāul's search is for the intangible, which dwells within rational being. God is in everything;therefore he is in life and in death, and as God is within the Bāul's being, the Bāul cannot separate life from death, or death from life. The scholastic explanation of the Bāul's approach to the life-death relationship is that the soul is allied to the self. For the Bāul's development the soul lives but the ego must die:

He who is able
to be born
at the door of death,
is devoted eternally . . .
Die before dying,
die living.[2]

Studying the Bāul songs, we find that the main theme, the interrelationship of forms, physical and mental, is wholly submerged within the formless, 'the one who moves close to his hands but away from his reach'. Therefore, the formless is the form, and the visible form the formless, beyond the senses of perception.

Reason is an inadequate tool when one is dealing with the intangible. One might just as well try to analyse the motive of a lover in falling in love; by the time the motive is explained, the feeling of love is in danger of death. Our life is balanced on this tightrope of knowing entwined with unknowing, of life with death; life is, to the Bāul, the condition of being locked within oneself while being free to accept that 'love, lust and the erotic acts are housed in one place'.

In assessing the rise and the development of the Bāul philosophy, we find that, like the Bāul belief, it drew upon any source that was available to it: the ancient pre-Aryan folklore of Bengal; the *Tantras*, which contained a mixture of pre-Aryan and

[1] Anonymous.

[2] By Gosāiñ Gopāl.

selected Aryan beliefs; the *Vedas*; the Buddhist rebellion against the Brahmans as an intellectual *élite*; the Vaishnava movement of Shri Chaitanya; and the introduction of Sūfī mysticism after the Islamic rule. The Bāul is not an intellectual but he has a natural wisdom which is simple and direct. Though he cannot read the doctrines, he is able to select and assimilate the essentials, and though he cannot accept the organized system, he accepts the faith. To the Bāul who is an individualist by nature, faith is spontaneous because it springs from natural trust. It is related to the *Adhar Mānush*, the unattainable man, who dwells in human form. Faith springs from an individual's feelings for the *Adhar Mānush*. Ritualized religion produces habits and customs which prevent one from being alert for the 'man of the heart'. Formalities threaten to become more important than God:

> God is deserting your temple
> As you amuse yourself
> By blowing conch-shells
> And ringing bells. . . .[1]

In his search for God, the Bāul is a determined individualist with a strong dislike of any organized system. The system stands in his way as threateningly as a road-block:

> The road to you is blocked
> By temples and mosques.
> I hear your call, my lord,
> But I cannot advance—
> Masters and teachers bar my way. . . .[2]

To the Bāul, God is with him everywhere he goes, but nowhere outside himself. He is always struggling to overcome his ego which separates him from the 'man of the heart':

> A man unknown to me
> And I,
> We both live together
> But with a gap
> Of millions of miles
> Between us. . . .[3]

[1] By Padmalochan. [2] By Madan [3] By Lālan.

Like a lover, God is always with the Bāul: at home and in distant lands, in scepticism and in trust, in desire and in feeling, in life and in death. The Bāul's songs reflect his efforts to understand freedom and at the same time to reconcile himself to the bondage of skin and bones.

DEBEN BHATTACHARYA

. . . All of us
In our different ways
Think of God.
He is the dispenser of love—
Beyond senses and feelings.

And yet,
It is only in the essence of loving,
That God is found. . . .

Anon

Scanning the cosmos
You waste your hours,
He is present
In this little vessel.

He does not dwell
In the complex of stars
Nor in limitless space;
He is not found
In the ethical scriptures
Nor in the text of the *Vedas.*
He lives beyond the existence
Of all.

The man is here
In his form without form
To adorn the hamlet of limbs,
And the sky above
Is the globe of his feelings—
The platform of spontaneous matter

Anon

Attested by your own heart,
O my master,
lead me the right way
as you play the melody
on the lute.
The lute could never sing
on its own,
without you to play it.

Anon

ೞ

Whom will you regard
as your teacher, O my heart,
and bow in reverence?
A teacher is a guest
at your own home
and a pedestrian out on the road.
Countless are the teachers, my heart,
for bowing in reverence.

The teacher is your offering dignity to all
and to the agony of death.
The teacher is the suffering in your own heart
that makes your eyes pour.
Whom will you regard with reverence
my heart?

Anon

ೞ

The ways of the tortuous river
Slip from your grasp.
Brothers, beware,
do not step into the stream.

The water rushes down
wrecking the blackened hills—
Brothers, beware
of the tortuous stream.

The river was dry
when the waters of the flood
surged down the tortuous stream.
How can we cross the river now?

Be on your guard, O boatman,
and hold tight to the oars.
And if the boat tends to turn over,
remember the master.

Anon

ꕤ

Only a connoisseur
of the flavours of love
can comprehend
the language of a lover's heart,
others have no clue.

The taste of lime
rests in the core of the fruit,
and even experts know
of no easy way
to reach it.

Honey is hidden
within the lotus bloom—
but the bee knows it.
Dung-beetles nestle in dung,
discounting honey.

The forest of Brindā
guards the essence of love—
Rādhā and Krishna,
with cowherds ruling the land.

Submission is the secret of knowledge.

Anon

Mad, mad,
we are all mad.
Why is this word
so derogatory then?
Diving deep into the heart's stream
you will find
that no one is better
than the one who is mad.

Some are mad after wealth
and others for glory.
Some go mad
with poverty,
and others with aesthetic forms,
the flavours of feelings.
Some are madly in love.
And some of those who go mad
only laugh or cry.
The glamour of madness is great.

Mad and mad!
Madness does not grow
on the tree—
but only when
the fake and the fact
are meaningless—
and all, being equal,
are bitter-sweet.

Anon

ꙮ

According to the views of the world, there is no one so undesirable and unworthy as he.

His heart locked with feelings, he is as gay as whirligig to the outside world. Cleaving wholly to his own nature, he laughs or cries, dances or begs as he wishes. Regardless of cleanliness or impurity, good or evil, his heart is carved in stone; but his life is a joy.

People grind their teeth at him, turn him away from their doorsteps when he goes begging for a handful of rice. He has no right to talk back as he must discard all for the sake of God, accepting all as part of divine caprice.

A tramp by nature and a beggar at that, he lives a strange life, almost insane, with values of his own which are contrary to those of others. His home being under the tree, he moves from district to district, all the year round, as a dancing beggar who owns nothing in the world but a ragged patch-work quilt.

Anon

ꙮ

The rites of spring
Have burst in the Tāj Mahal.
The meaning of the words
Right and wrong
Are cast away into the empty space
Of meaninglessness.
The rites of spring
Have entered the Tāj Mahal.
Little sons of pigs
Who are ruled by the powerful king
Have taken charge of all.
The rites of spring
Have burst in the Tāj Mahal.

Anon[1]

ꙮ

Nothing has happened
and nothing will happen.
What is there, is there.

I became a king
in my dream
and my subjects
occupied the entire earth.
I sat on the throne
ruling like a lion,
living a happy life.
The world obeyed me.

[1] Tape-recorded in Calcutta, 1954. Singers: Ramakrishna Bāul Sangha, Howrah.

As I turned in my bed,
all was clear:
I was not a lion
but a lion's uncle,
a jackass,
the village idiot. . . .

Anon

ꝏ

Come if you wish to meet
The novel man.
He has abandoned
His worldly possessions
For the beggar's sack
That hangs from his shoulder.
He speaks of the eternal mother
[Kāli, the goddess of time]
Even as he enters the Ganges.

Simple words can overcome
Ignorance and disbelief:
Kāli and Krishna are one.
The words may differ—
The meaning is precisely the same.
He who has broken
The barrier of words,
Has conquered limits:
Allah or Jesus, Moses or Kāli,
The rich or the poor,
Sage or fool,
All are one and the same to him.

Lost in his own thoughts,
He seems insane to others.
He opens his arms
To welcome the world,
Calling all to the ferry boat
Tied to the coast of life.

Anon[1]

[1] Tape-recorded in Calcutta, 1954. Singers: Ramakrishna Bāul Sangha, Howrah.

Commit yourself to the earth
while on the earth,
my heart,
if you wish to attain
the unattainable man.[1]
Place at his feet
your flowers of feelings
and the prayers of tears
flooding your eyes.

The man you seek
is earthed
in the earth,
deceased while being.

Dying with death,
you must live to seek. . . .

Anon

ꕤ

Raise the torch of love
as high as the lightning
to know the precious gold
from common tin.

Words of wisdom
describing God
can reveal no riches
in a darkened room.
Seeking in darkness
is confusing. . . .

Break the barriers,
the nights of darkness,
and look at the sky:
The shapeless is held
as a beautiful form
in the arms of the moon. . . .[2]

Anon

[1] God.

[2] *Chandra*, the moon, representing Krishna.

. . . The potter
cuts the clay
and kneads it
and shapes it
until it is elegant.

Impure gold
holds no colour on its own.
You must burn it on fire
for purity
and colour. . . .

Anon

ꝏ

O my senseless heart,
you have failed to cultivate
the human-land.
How will you face the tax claims
when the season escapes?
You have no balance
to your credit at all.

As you wonder sitting alone,
the time approaches for death,
heedless of all.
O my insane heart,
you have travelled
eight million times
the painful ways of life to death,[1]
to find the measured land,
the body of the man.
Why did you let such human-earth
turn to waste-land?
Cultivated,
it could have yielded a harvest of gold.

[1] These lines relate to the conception of re-birth, through various stages of human development.

Take up, my heart,
the spade of devotion—
wrench out the weeds of sin.
The seed of faith will grow.[1]

Passions within you
are feeding on you.
They will never let you act.
Leave them and worship
Shri Gaurānga's feet,
the root of devotion and love.

Anon[2]

ꕥ

You must be single-minded
to visit the court of my Gaurchānd—
[the prophet of devotion and love]
If your mind is torn into two
you will swim in a quandary
and never reach the shore.

The court has ordered the queen of love,
Rādhā, to ferry all across,
but after the mind is measured.
The jewellers who weigh are strict
and the scales are accurate. . . .

Anon[3]

ꕥ

How could he stand
in a normal, upright way—
the man without
a heart in him?

[1] *Bījamantra*—the charged-words, or a set of selected letters from Sanskrit alphabet, handed down by the master to the disciple. This is also known as the "seed-words". By repeating and concentrating on the *mantra*, the disciple is expected to co-ordinate his physical, mental and psychic nature through which the cosmic power reveals itself.

[2] Tape-recorded in Siuri, Birbhum. Singer: Purna Chandra, son of Nabanidās Bāul.

[3] Tape-recorded in Siuri, Birbhum. Singer: Nabanidās Bāul.

The roots of his tree
are planted in the sky
and the branches
lie on the earth.
Flowers are in blossom
on the tree
but it never bears fruit.
The fruit is
in the hand of God.

For him the river
is dying of thirst
and the fire perishes,
freezing,
and birds nestle in the water. . . .

He is meeting his master
in the cremation ground.

Anon

ꕥ

What dealings
Can you ever conclude
With someone
Who is unaware
Of the feelings
In loving. . . .

The owl
Stares at the sky—
Sitting blind
To the rays
Of the sun. . . .

Anon

ꕥ

. . . He is watching the path
With a balance in hand.

3 *Anandalahari*

Be bold, my heart,
And enter the territory
Of the great
By daring the unconquerable.
Let desires be at your will,
Obeying you.

The path is perilous—
A narrow float
Divides the wild waters of the sea.
And submarine chains
Bar the way
To the rowing boats.

You must also cross
The moat of fire,
And walk on the edge of a sword
In steady steps.
Below you lie the death of pain
And a furnace of fire. . . .

Anon

ꩡ

Dear Love,
You who share my pain,
Can tell me why my heart
Is lost to listlessness
And walks on its own
Toward its own self,
With no hue and cry.

There is no patience
In the core of my heart—
Shivering with tears
It cries with the eyes,
And in the silence of lovely sound
Forever calls:
Come, please come.

Anon

What colour is your cottage
On the shore of this bogus world?
The frame of your home is made of bones
And the roof is thatched with skin.
But the pair of peacocks
On the landing-pier,
Hardly know that
They will end one day.

As the childhood passed in play
Passes the age of passion-sport.
The old age too is going away
Calling, calling,
For the master and the lord.
Your teeth are dropping down
And the hair is going grey.
The age of manhood
Is at a low ebb.
The plaster of your painted home
Will be crumbling now—
Softly, softly.

Anon[1]

ꕥ

If you wish to board an aeroplane,
you must travel light
to be safe from the danger of a crash.
You must renounce
your errors and inhibitions
and show your credentials in the aerodrome.
Paying your fare of devotion to God,
you must give up
your worldly wealth
to buy a ticket for the seat.

[1] Tape-recorded in Calcutta, 1954. Singer: Abbass-uddin, a professional singer of folk songs.

The feet of your master,
the aeroplane,
will take you to Vishnu's sphere,[1]
even before an eyelid's wink. . . .

Anon[2]

ꕥ

That astounding engine
of the train
makes the wheels move
with organized power
from the beautiful earth,
fire, water and air.

But the day comes when
the passenger goes,
and the boiler breaks down
and the engine stops
and four shoulders
bear the machinery
to the funeral ground.
And all for the astounding engine
of the train. . . .

Anon[3]

ꕥ

O, my heart,
Let us go then
On a promenade
To the grove
Of Krishna's love.
The breeze
Of joy
Will calm
Your life.

[1] The preserving Power of the Hindu Triple-Forces, the other two being Brahmā and Shiva, for creation and dissolution respectively.
[2] Tape-recorded in Varanasi. Singer: Haripada Debnath.
[3] Tape-recorded in Varanasi. Singer: Haripada Debnath.

In that woodland
Eternally bloom
Five scented flowers.[1]
Their fragrance
Will enchant
Your life and soul,
Giving them
Sovereign dignity. . . .

Ananta

ꙮ

Who gave shape
to such a splendid room,
with astonishing workmanship?
The master-builder
merits my gratitude
but where does he himself live?

The room erected
on three colonnades[2]
is a network
of rope, cord and string.[3]
It has nine standard doors[4]
but the windows[5]
are countless.
The span of the room,
fourteen quarter-measures,[6]
can contain
full fourteen worlds. . . .[7]

[1] The five elements—earth, water, fire, air and ether.

[2] Two legs and the spinal column of the physical body and *Idā*, *Pingalā* and *Shushumnā* vessels of the spiritual body.

[3] Three and a half *koti*, meaning 35 million—blood-vessels, arteries, veins etc.

[4] The nine forces of perception and action: ears, skin, eyes, nose, anus, genital organ, hands, feet and the tongue (representing the double function of tasting and speaking).

[5] The pores of the skin.

[6] *Choudda poyā*, fourteen quarter-measures, is the popular expression to represent three and a half times the length of a person's forearm, which is considered to be the approximate height of a man or a woman.

[7] *Saptapātāl* and *saptalok*: Seven nether-worlds are represented by the lower half of the human body, and six heavenly spheres and the earth by the upper half.

Amazing workmanship
of the master-mechanic!
The room revolves
and halts on its own—
mobility alternates
with motionlessness.

Talking earth
walling my room,
holds fire and water
in a united stream,
flushing the floor.
In my room
live in total unity
the sage and the thief,
the demon and the man—
poison and nectar. . . .

Ananta

ഌ

The heart, a lotus,
Continue flowering
Age after age.
You are bound to it
And so am I,
And with no escape.
The lotus blossoms,
Blossoms, blossoms,
There is no end to it.
But all these lotuses
Have one type of honey,
With one particular taste.

The bee is avid
And unable to leave.
So, you are bound
And I am bound—
Where is freedom then?

Bishā Bhuñimāli

The essence of love
lies in carnal lust
bearing a deep secret.
Only lovers
can unravel it. . .

Chandidās Gosāiñ

ꕥ

Each fruit is open to
two frontiers
and borne on
a pair of trees.[1]
Deep meditation
reveals the knowledge
beyond any doubt. . . .

The two
who are wholly present,
can bring forth a fruit
to offer the master.
They are conscious
and fruitful.

Darkness and copper.[2]
The well never sinks
into the water. . . .

Chandidās Gosāiñ

ꕥ

Human limbs
are held together
by a pair of lotus blooms
growing in the
lower and the upper regions
of the body
but the lotuses
burst open and shut
as the sun
in the body
rises and sets.

[1] The male and the female elements.

[2] Offering of copper to the darkness. Implying that the darkness is a blessing for the well.

On which of these blooms
is the full moon born
and on which the darkest
night of the month?

On which of these lotuses
rests the total eclipse
of the sun
and the moon. . . ?

Chandidās Gosāiñ

ಣ

Let ripeness appear
In its own time,
For the full flavour
Of the fruit.
A green jackfruit
Can be softened by blows
But not made sweet. . . .

Chandidās Gosāiñ

ಣ

The milk of the lioness
is seen at its best
when stored in a golden cup.

Worshipping prospers
in a proper container.
The lover
who wholly loves
can reach reality,
comprehending the unattainable man.
The secrets of death
are revealed to him
while he is fully alive.
What does he care
for the other shores of life . . .?

Chandidās Gosāiñ

The master of the universe
belongs to no one
but you must know him.
As you explore your mind
looking for him,
feelings override thoughts.

Appearing, vanishing,
again and again,
breathing life into life,
he who is the life
Of the life's hidden riches,
eats at the life. . . .

Chandidās Gosāiñ

ꕥ

My worries continue
for my crumbling boat
that can no longer carry—
water rushes through her hulk
and salt eats at her keel.

My boat can bear no more
the burden of water.
O master of my life,
open your eyes,
show me your kindness
and hold me as I die.
I can never be
in 'me' again.

There lay the river Hooghly
as I moored my boat
reaching the jetty at Kālnā.
I cast the anchor deep.
Passions like bandits
leapt at me,
raided my boat
and went off with the spoils.
They cut the mooring rope
and left me adrift.

The master says:
wash away
the stains of your heart,
and your boat will thrive,
in tranquillity.

Chiru

ꩡ

My unknowing heart,
Can you not lay the snare
That catches the moon?

Your eyes are dilated
By your whirligigs
As you try to seize
The sky at one single leap. . . .

Dīn

ꩡ

Never plunge
into the river of lust,
you will not reach the shores.
It is a river of no coasts
where typhoons rage. . . .

Dwija Kailāshchandra

ꩡ

Go to the home
of beauty and form,
should you wish to see
the man within. . . .

His ways cross
the sphere
where life lives with death
and sense with insanity.
Close your eyes and
try to catch him,
He is slipping by. . . .

Erfān Shāh

To find nectar,
Stir the cauldron
On the fire—
And unite the act of loving
With the feeling for love.

Distill the sweetness
Of the heart
And reach the treasures,
Devoting yourself
To those wholly devoted.

Sweetness rests
In the moon[1]
And sweet nectar
In flowers. . . .

Erfān Shāh

ಐ

My soul cries out,
Caught in the snare of beauty
Of the formless one.
As I cry by myself,
Night and day,
Beauty amassed before my eyes
Surpasses numerous moons and suns.
If I look at the clouds in the sky,
I see his beauty afloat;
And I see him walk on the stars
Blazing my heart. . . .

Fikirchānd

ಐ

My life is a little oil lamp
Floating on the waves.
But from which landing-pier
Did you set me afloat?

[1] Krishna.

With darkness ahead of me
and darkness behind,
Darkness overlaps my night—
While the necklace of waves
Constantly rings.
The storm of the night
Relentlessly flows
Below the stars,
And the lamp is afloat
On the shoreless space—
As my company. . . .

Gangārām

ꕥ

The eyes see
And the skin feels
The dust and the dirt.
Tasted on the tongue of life,
The lord of love is true.
Flowers of form
And the flavours of love
Blossom and wilt,
But where lies the string of feeling?
My lord is playing his flute
out of the doors,
As I restlessly ache
Listening to him.
I could not gather
The garland of meeting
And in shame I walk my way.
I go farther and farther away
And yet still I hear the tune.

What good is distance for a serving soul—
The world is a city of my lord.
He is the sea
And the river as well
As the chief of the landing-stage.

Gangārām

What is the use of calling someone who does not respond? What evidence do I have that he can hear my heart?

No one can describe his shape or his complexion, yet everyone is busy talking about him, making special announcements. I laugh as I hear.

I have never seen him since my birth. How do I know whether he exists or not? As I can see, they all appear to grope in darkness, trying to reach him.

Some say that he lives in the heaven. Others say that his home is not to be known. I hear them but every single statement leaves me more and more confused.

Hoping to find him some pray. Some go to pilgrimage, and others fast. Some become vegetarians, others wear the ochre-coloured robes of the monks.

The Mussalmans call him Allah and the Christians Jesus Christ. The Hindus call him Bhagavān. I have no doubt that they are one.

Judging all the points, I feel that God exists on its own, immensely, immeasurably, but adorned with shapes. The ocean or a drop of water, each is in God; each of them shines with its own brilliance within God.

Gobinda Dās

ꙮ

I often repeat the word 'I' but who is the 'I' within myself I am not sure.

My 'I' eats no rice or vegetables, savouries or sweets, butter or cheese.

Expensive shawls are not for my 'I'. Colourful jackets or shirts are useless. Even a scrap of loin-cloth is not needed.

This 'I' has no peerage or any profession. It is not a lawyer or an advocate, a district magistrate or a porter, a handyman or a butler.

It is neither a sage nor a monk, neither a householder nor an ascetic living in the forest. This 'I' has no desire for the day-to-day ritual of the righteous living.

As 'I' is the very basis of spirituality, worships, prayers or meditations are superfluous for it.

This 'I' is not locked into one dwelling. Its relationship

with the body resembles that of the bird with the tree. The bird lives on the tree but does not grow on it.

The 'I' is not concerned with love or hate, and yet it is intimate with all beings.

This 'I' is like a conjurer, able to assume a multitude of characters in many garments. But when removed from one, it returns to its origin.

And there, it needs no name such as Gaur, Gadāi or Gopikānta, Keshab or Kenārām; or surnames or titles. It has no trace of caste, class or race.

Gobne Dās
(possibly Gobinda Dās)

ᔓᔕ

That enchanting river
Reflects the very form
Of the formless one.
Sense the essence of the matter,
My undiscerning heart,
And feel the taste
On your tongue.

You see only
A little ditch of life
And remain involved with it
In drunken stupor. . . .

Gopāl

ᔓᔕ

. . . The leaves are bejewelled
By the moon[1]
As you can see,
But where, my heart,
Are the roots
Of the plant?

[1] Krishna.

On which water
Floats the lotus bloom
Where sits your teacher?
Gazelles leap
About the lotus pond
And the black-bee stings thc bloom.

Gopāl

ဢ

God has reversed the acts
Of the play:

The land talks
In paradox
And the flowers devour
The heads of fruits,
And the gentle vine,
Roaring,
Strangles the tree.
The moon rises in the day
And the sun at night
With shining rays. . . .

The blood is white,
And on the lake of blood
Float a pair of swans
Copulating continuously
In a jungle of lust and love. . . .

Gopāl

ဢ

Sown on a slab of stone,
The seed of faith[1]
Dries day by day
Never sprouting.
You may cultivate
The arid earth
But the hardened seed
Will yield no harvest.

[1] *Bījamantra*, see note p. 47.

Great is the woodland
Where the sandal grows,
And the breeze, bearing
The scent of sandal,
Perfumes the neighbouring trees,
Turning them into sandalwood. . . .

Gosāiñ Charan

ꙮ

. . . Forget not
that your body contains
the whole of existence.

Gosāiñ Gopāl

ꙮ

When the confluence
of the three rivers [1]
(body, mind and spirit)
dries out,
and the great fish,[2]
preserver Vishnu's
first expression of life
vanishes away,
death's god detains you.

Wild illusions
confuse your path to reality,
making you forget
what the teacher had taught you.
Day by day
your days slip by
into lethargy.
If you wish to hold
the moon in your hands,
clip the noose
around your neck,
and worship love.

[1] *Tribeni,* see note p. 75.

[2] *Min,* see note p. 92.

The teacher is the *Mīn*,[1]
the first to find life
in the turbulent junction
of the three rivers,
billowing high waves.
If you wish to contact
the great fish of life,
be aware.
If careless,
you will encounter death.

Shut the doors
on the face of lust.
Attain the greatest,
the unattainable man,[2]
and act
as the lovers act.
Meet the death
before you die.

Gosāiñ Gopāl

ꕥ

The man that breathes,
lives on the air,
and the other, unseen,
rests above reach.
Between the two,
moves another man
as a secret link.
Worship knowingly.

It is a sport
amongst the three of them.
My searching heart,
whom do you seek?

[1] *Mīn*, see note 92.
[2] *Adhar mānush*, meaning the supreme man unattainable by the senses, God.

Purna Chandra Bāul (with *ānandalahari*) and Sudhā Bāul (with the lute *dotārā*) 4

Bāul instruments 5

Between the doors
of birth and death,
stands yet another door,
wholly inexplicable.
He who is able
to be born
at the door of death,
is devoted eternally. . . .

Die before dying,
die living.

Gosāiñ Gopāl

ꩧ

Reaching for reality
is lame talk
to describe the goal
of the lover-worshipper. . . .

He will attain
the great unattainable,
stare at the face
of the invisible one,
bearing the nectar of love. . . .

Gosāiñ Gopāl

ꩧ

Where is the home
of the moon?
And what makes
the cycle of the days
wander encircling
the moving nights?

The lunar eclipse
in the night of the full moon
is known to all.
But no one enquires
about the blackened moon
on the darkest night
of the month. . . .

He who is able to make
the full moon rise
in the sky
of the darkest night,
has a right to claim
the glory of the three worlds—
the heaven, the earth
and the nether-spheres. . . .

Gosāiñ Gopāl

꩜

The rites of ferocious love
Rest in the essence of
Supreme beauty
And the dignity of the *yoga*,[1]
As the connoisseur knows.

Awarding his hands
To the fangs of a snake
Fearless, he lives.
Poison and ambrosia
Of the immortal life
Are one and the same
Thing to him.
He is dead
While wholly living.

The essence of beauty
In the mirror of love
Stares at his face—
The formless
Within the visible form.
The fire cools
In his hands
And quick-silver roosts
On flames. . . .

Guruchānd

[1] *Yoga* means union, the path to the unity of body, mind, and spirit through physical and mental discipline.

I am forbidden to reveal
The secret of my heart
But my life
Can no longer be,
Seeking empathy.
Danger threatens my life
If I fail to know
The nature of the heart
That shares my pains. . . .

Love springs
As feelings merge—
Divided forms
Assume a single way.
A pair of hearts
Running in parallel streams,
Long to reach the god of loving. . . .

Haridās

ꙮ

Will the day ever dawn
when the treasured man[1]
of my heart
will become my own?
Though not cast
in any shape,
the man is evidenced
in the ways of love.

Those who are absorbed
by the flavours of feelings,
and are wholly living
with the knowledge of death,
have won their foes—
pride and envy,
lust and anger,
ignorance and greed.

[1] God.

If your life, flowing with life,
longs for the man,
the man will come
with kindly steps.
Look at the worlds
of god, demon and man
[all held in your body]—
He is already there. . . .

Haridās

ꙮ

Those who are dead
and yet fully alive
and know the flavours
and feelings
in loving;
they will cross the river.
Gazing at
the stream of life and death,
they seek integrity.
They have no wish
for happiness at all,
walking against the wind.

They kill lust
with lust
and enter the city of love,
unattached. . . .

Haridās

ꙮ

Free impulses
live together with
the forces of abstinence,
and the feminine energy
entwined with the spirit of man
resemble the tuned strings
and the lute,
wholly indivisible.
The heart is the home
of no-separation. . . .

Hāude Gosāiñ

He who knows
The essence of love,
Fears none.
Devoted only to
Love's own form
Alive before his eyes,
His home is in
Happiness itself. . . .

Lulling lust
By lust alone,
He raids the heart
Of the god that churns all hearts,[1]
Finding himself
In perennial love.

Hāude Gosāiñ

How can you walk
The ways of love,
Carrying stolen loot
With impunity?

In the forest of Brinda[2]
[Where Krishna led the lovers]
Loving is worshipping.
The riches raised from rubbish
Are measured with care
In a jeweller's balance.
The land is ruled by women
With lovers as their vassals.
The greedy and lusting thieves
Are outlawed, enchained.

As the essence of purity[3]
In the brilliance of the sky,

[1] Manmatha.

[2] Brindāban, a town in North India where Krishna spent his days as a youth.

[3] *Vishuddha-chakra,* one of the six symbolic lotus blooms representing the stages in the spiritual body of the man, is placed in the throat, and is of sixteen petals in smoke-grey. It represents purity.

Love transcends lust,
Evolving ecstasy.
The bellows breathe
Into the fire of life
And stabilize mercury. . . .

Hāude Gosāiñ

ꙮ

When the life,
The mind,
And the eyes
Are in agreement,
The target is
Within your reach:
You can see
The formless *Brahma*
With bare eyes. . . .

Hāude Gosāiñ

ꙮ

On the other shore
Of the ocean
Of one's own self,
Quivers a drop of fluid—
As the origin of all.
But who can cross the seas
To reach it?

The root of all[1]
Is based in you.
Explore the base
To reach the essence. . . .

Hāude Gosāiñ

[1] *Mūlādhāra-chakra,* the first of the six stages of man's spiritual body is represented by a lotus of four petals, placed between the anus and the genital organ. It is regarded as the symbol for respiration and life in Yogic terms.

Release the sensation
of taste
on your tongue.
Open the doors of feeling
for beloved Krishna—
the image of eternal love.
Nectar, showering
on the lotus of spontaneity,
runs down the stem
of the bloom
to be one with the water
where flowers lie. . . .

Lust and love
and the erotic acts
are housed in one single place
where sorrows and joys
do not exist. . . .

Hāude Gosāiñ

ꕥ

Light has burst
On the walls of the sky;
The kind one has blossomed at last.
Waking in the morning
I saw him present,
Appearing close to my face.

Flowers wither and birds flutter
And the dew forms on the leaves.
The glow of the night is melting away
With the rising heat of the sun.
The kind one is the light of the moon.
Ishān cries as he ponders over these
With a sense
Of deep pain.

Ishān Jugi

My lord is not a broken wheel
that squeals every minute. . . .

Tell me, my silent master,
O my lord,
What worship may open me
to *Brahma's* lotus bloom.
The stars and the moon eternally move,
with no sound at all.
Each cycle of the universe
in silence prays,
welling up with the essence of love.

Ishān Jugi

ഩ

My heart is saturated
but I wish I knew with what—
joy or death.
What good is there in my calling God
as I no longer fall for future or past?
My heart dances with the unique joy—
that his anklet-bells
jingle night and day.

A sense of wonder has overtaken all:
where is that ocean
and where are the rivers?
And yet still the waves are there
for you to observe,
only if you unite your eyes
with your heart.
If you wish to view such spectacular play,
mingle your heart
with the eyes of your heart.

Ishān Jugi

ഩ

I am fulfilled
Being a blow of your own breath—
On your flute.

I am not sad
If I end with one single tune.
Your flute is the universe
Of three different worlds,
of god, demon and man,
And I am the blow of your breath.

Tuned to your finger-holes,
Right or wrong,
I sound through sleepless nights.
I sound through the months
Of monsoon and the spring,
But together with your heart.

I have no sadness at all
If I completely end.
What more can I wish for me
Than being blown away with such melody.

Ishān Jugi

ᨐ

How can I capture the man[1]
Who is not to be caught.

He lives on the other bank
Of the river,[2]
And the skin of my eyes
Screens my sight. . . .

Jādubindu

ᨐ

Blind one,
How can you stumble
On a straight,
Spontaneous path?[3]

[1] *Adhar mānush*, the uncaptureable man, represents the Bāul's god.

[2] The river *Birajā*. Birajā was one of the secret loves of Krishna. When Rādhā came to know about this affair, Birajā, abandoning life, changed into a river. The Bāuls consider the other bank of the river Birajā as heaven.

[3] *Sahaja*, meaning inborn, spontaneous. The *Sahaja* path represents a religious movement within the fold of Vaishnavism. See *Love Songs of Chandidās*, Deben Bhattacharya, London, 1967.

Be spontaneous
In your own self,
And find the way
That is born in you. . . .

Jādubindu

ꕥ

Pour out
the useless cloudy fluid,
O angry tapper.
Hacking at a date-palm tree
is not tapping it.

The tapper of love
works his way up
to the top of the tree,
aided by the mind,
the supporting strap,
tied in a loop
around the date-palm.

Piercing the heart
with a sharp-edged knife,
he opens the course
in torrents of
sweet, crystal juice. . . .

Jādubindu

ꕥ

Look, look for him
In the temple of your limbs.
He is there
As the lord of the world,
Speaking,
Singing,
In enchanting tunes.
He is an expert
At hide-and-seek,
No one can see him.
He is the universe
With no form of his own. . . .

Do not try to catch him,
O my heart,
He can never be caught.
You can only hope for him
In whole faith. . . .

Jādubindu

ꕥ

I plunged into the water
like a fisherman,
hoping to catch
the fish of faith.
Devotion
which was my fishing net,
got torn into pieces.

I only gathered
some useless shells—
jealousies and blames,
churning the mud
in vain. . . .

Jādubindu

ꕥ

Tribeni,[1]
the perilous confluence
of the three rivers,
penetrates the nether-world,
causing instant death
if you step into it.
In a raging typhoon,
the tidal waves
with the ebbing water
flow concurrently,
night and day.

[1] *Tribeni* is the confluence of the Ganges, the Jamuna and the Saraswati at Prayag, near Allahabad in North India. But the Bāuls use the term *Tribeni* in a metaphysical sense, implying the meeting ground of body, mind and spirit; of heaven, earth and nether-world; of desire, love and the devotion to God, etc.

You cannot row a boat
in this shoreless ocean.
Saints are dying in it,
and the gods drowning. . . .

Speechlessly,
the sages and the seekers gaze
at the river-line
as it bends away
with the horizon. . . .

Jādubindu

ꕥ

Plough-man,
are you out of your wits
not to take care
of your own land?

A squadron of six birds[1]
is picking at the rice,
grown golden and ripe,
in the field of your limbs.

Farming the splendid,
measured land
of this human body,
you raised the crop,
the devotion to God.
But passions eat at it
like sparrows.

The fence of consciousness
is down to dust,
leaving open gaps.
Cattle clamber up
and feast on your harvest. . . .

Jādubindu[2]

[1] The six enemies or the weaknesses of man: lust, anger, greed, ignorance, pride and envy.

[2] Tape-recorded in Siuri, Birbhum. Singer: Purna Chandra, son of Nabanidās Bāul.

Shame to you,
my shameless heart,
what now can I say?
You have gathered a piece of glass
at the price of gold.
In spite of a pair of eyes,
you missed the valuable jewels,
caring only for artificial stones.
Wandering blindfolded,
you could not see
that the house overflowed
with the choicest rubies,
and diamonds,
and gems of fire.

Hugging a sickle
in your waist-band,
what do you search
from field to field?
What is the use?
My heart,
will you not explore for once,
the home of beauty. . . ?

Jādubindu

ꕥ

If you fail to recognize
Your own heart,
Can you ever come to know
The great unknown?

The farthest away
Will be nearest to you,
And the unknown
Within your knowing. . . .

Fill up your home
With the world abroad,
And you will attain
The unattainable man. . . .

Kālāchānd

The body of man
is a land for wish-fulfilling—
care will produce
a harvest of jewels.
Plough it in a propitious time.
Hopes that ushered you
to this material world
will bear fruit.

Action is the steel
for making your plough;
passions are oxen.
Sow your seeds on a ready land,
treasures will be yours
at the harvest time. . . .

Kālāchānd

The primeval man,
called the imperishable,
is eternally aloft.
His form as
subtle as infinity,
treks emptiness,
it roams the nought—
the universe of nothing.

His will produced
one primal drop [1]
[the minute as the immense],
which bore the seed
and the flower
and the fruit,
all in the nature
of one single drop. . . .

Kālāchānd

[1] *Bindu*, the drop, the point of emergence and dissolution, representing the whole.

Gay and glorious
to the eyes,
the flower opens
in a world of colours
and yet remains unshaped. . . .

Poison encircles the bloom
but the devout eats the venom
and digests it.
The flower opens to be seen
all the year round. . . .

Kānāi

ꙮ

Let your heart be a caring home
For the man of your heart.

Focus your vision
Through the eye-black
Of loving,
he will be floating
On the mercurial mirror. . . .

. . . Hours wither
Like broken games
On the playground of the earth.
Abandon search
And join the carnival of love.

Kānāilāl

ꙮ

. . . Poison that kills the man
can cure the man too
depending on the physician's skill.
'That which gives life
gives death',
is the maxim for worshipping God. . . .

Krishnadās

Formless,
The flower floats.
But where is the plant?
And the water?
Yet still, the flower
Eternally floats
On the waves
Of life.
The bees buzzing,
Drink its honey
While Lālan,
Seeking, chasing,
Misses the flower.

Lālan

❧

And as yet
The heart of my heart
Knows no better:
Where am I
And where shall I be
And when
With whom.

The futile words
'My house, my home'
Are raised to dust
As the eyelids blink.

While dreams mount
The layers of bricks
Of my mansion house,
My foolish heart
Marches to its own funeral
Without even knowing it. . . .

Lālan

6 Nabanidās Bāul, in meditation

Never in my life
Did I once face
The man who lives
In my own little room.[1]

My eyes, blinded
By the weight of storms,
Can see nothing,
Even when he stirs.
My hands fail
To reach his hands
As he is forever engaged
With the world.

I keep silent
When they call him
The bird of life,
And the water
And the fire
And the earth
And the air,
While no one is sure.

Could I ever wish
To know any one else?
I do not yet know
My own little room. . . .

Lālan

ꩡ

No words can describe the *chātaka*,[2]
the rain-bird's love
for the cloud
and its water.

[1] The body.

[2] In Indian poetry and painting, the *chātaka*, or *Hierococcyx varius*, is depicted as the bird which is intensely in love with the clouds and lives on rain-water.

Clouds deceive it so
and yet, flies the bird,
eager to seize,
gazing, gazing at the clouds,
never blinking.

The way of all *chātakas*
is the death of thirst.
They will not drink
unless clouds break. . . .

Lālan

ꕥ

I have no knowledge
of my own self.
If for once I could know
what I am,
the unknown would be known.
God is near by
and yet far away,
like the mountain hiding
behind my screening hair.
I travel distant towns
of Dacca and Delhi,
constantly searching
but circling round my own knees.
God is alive
in my living form,
only purity of heart
will lead me to him.
The more I study
the wisdom of the *Vedas*
the more I am bewildered,
repeating 'I'.
O my heart,
seek shelter at his feet—
he who knows the word 'I'.

Lālan says:
with a confused heart,
I am blind
in spite of my eyes.

Lālan[1]

ꕥ

Can I ever again be born as a man?
Hurry up, my heart,[2]
and act as you wish
in this world.

God has created man
in immortal form,
wishing to be human.
Nothing is better than man.

Great is your luck,
my heart,
to become the boat
of human life.

Follow the current
and set sail.
Do not sink,
the boat is filled.

The human shape
is made by God
since man can pray
only loving.[3]

Do not miss the shores
nor lose the sail. . . .

Lālan

[1] Tape-recorded in Calcutta, 1954. Singer: Bhatktadās Bāul. See record No. BAM–LD 099, *Religious Songs from Bengal*, Paris, 1966.

[2] *Mon*, springing from the Sanskrit word *manas*, in colloquial Bengali, it implies both heart and mind. For the Bāul, the *mon* represents himself symbolising the mind and the heart, spirit and matter.

[3] *Mādhurya* represents the sweet and loving aspect of God according to Vaishnava classification.

My heart is not
To my heart's liking.
I wish I knew
How to unite the two. . . .

Lālan

ꕥ

I wish to go to Kāshi.[1]
The noose of *karma*[2]
Closing round my neck,
makes me move
In a carrousel.
My foolish heart
Brought me to this state,
Near disaster.
My boat will
Certainly sink
In the narrow waterways
Of being born
And born again. . . .

Lālan

ꕥ

This land offered me
Only dubious joys,
Where else may I go?
I found a broken boat
And my life got busy
Scooping water out. . . .

Lālan

ꕥ

How long shall it be
Before I can see the moon,[3]
Removing the darkness
Of my heart?

[1] Kāshi, Vārānasi, or Benares, is a Hindu pilgrimage because of the Ganges.

[2] *Karma* means action, work or deed, the effect of which continues beyond the immediate time of one life.

[3] *Adhar-chānd,* the unattainable moon, sometimes referred to as the unattainable man, is the Bāul's god.

That kind moon
Who brought me to this world.
What prayers may I offer to him
And what meditations?
Shall I go to *Kāshi* for a pilgrimage[1]
Or stay in a forest?
O where shall I go
To find my moon. . . . ?

Lālan

꩜

My heart,
you are in a muddle.
As the days go,
your inherited riches,
plundered, fly.
You only doze
around the clock
drinking dreams[2]
and living in five homes[3]
with no control.

The robber rests with you,
my heart,
in your own room
but how can you know?
Your eyes are shut
in sleep. . . .

Lālan

꩜

Please, Kānāi,[4]
come to *Vraja* for once
to see the state of the land,
and how your mother Jashodā fares.

[1] Varanasi, or Benares.
[2] Illusion.
[3] The five elements—earth, water, fire, air and ether.
[4] Kānāi is a diminutive term for Krishna.

Father Nanda, pained at your parting,
is blinded by tears,
and your cowherd friends
are thrown into confusion.

The young and the aged
are constantly joyless,
longing to be at your precious feet.
The animals and the birds
are restless, fitful
not hearing your flute sing.

Lālan

ꕥ

What is the colour of your love,
O my insane heart,
That you wish to renounce the world
As an ascetic
For Islam?
The Hindus and Muslims
Are sundered into two.
The Muslims aspire
To their particular heaven
Named *behest*
And the Hindus dwell on theirs
Called *svarga*.
Both these words,
Like formal gates,
Lifeless.
Who cares for them . . . ?

Lālan

ꕥ

Poison and nectar
Are mingled in one—
like music
Played and heard
In one single act.

The human heart
Free from flaw,
Forever enlightened,
Sees good and evil
Same time,
Same place.

A child sucking his mother
Draws milk,
A leech at the breasts of a woman
Draws blood. . . .

Lālan

ꕥ

Who is there for you
to call your own,
my heart?
For whom do you shed
your futile tears?

Brothers and friends—
let them be;
the world is there.
Your own dear life
is hardly your own. . . .

You have come alone,
you will go alone. . . .

Lālan

ꕥ

A man unknown to me
And I,
We live together
But in a void—
A million miles
Between us.

My eyes blindfolded
By worldly dreams,
Cannot recognize him,
Or see. . . .

Lālan

ೞ

He talks to me
But he would not let me see him.
He moves
Close to my hands
But away from my reach.
I explore
The sky and the earth
Searching him,
Circling round my error
Of not knowing me:
Who am I
And who is he?

Lālan

ೞ

As the man and the woman in me
Unite in love,
The brilliance of beauty
Balanced on the bi-petalled
Lotus bloom in me[1]
Dazzles my eyes.
The rays
Outshine the moon
And the jewels
Glowing on the hoods of snakes.[2]

My skin and bone
Are turned to gold.
I am the reservoir of love,
Alive as the waves.

[1] *Dvidal,* the two-petalled lotus bloom, refers to one of the six centres of the spiritual body. See notes pp. 69–70. In order to make the meaning clear, the translator has added the first two lines in the verse.

[2] According to Bengali legends, the most precious jewel in the world is found on the hood of certain poisonous snakes.

A single drop of water
Has grown into a sea,
Unnavigable. . . .

Lālan

ꙮ

The moon is encircled by moons.[1]
How can I hold it
In my hands?
The unseizable moon,[2]
Glowing in the brilliance
Of a million moons,
Rocks my head
In a lunar carnival. . . .

Moon fruits adorn
The tree of the moon,
Flashing,
Luminously flashing.

I try to see
But my eyes cannot bear;
The rays of beauty
Dazzle them.

Lālan

ꙮ

Pandemonuim broke loose
in the guard-room of love.
My heart was caught
like a thief
by the greatest of lovers[3]
who had set snares
in the air. . . .

Lālan

[1] This song appears similar to Vaishnava poems expressing Rādhā and Krishna's dazzling beauty. [2] *Adhar-chānd*, see note p. 84.

[3] *Rasik*, a connoisseur of the essence of feelings, is an adjective often attributed to Krishna.

The key to my own home
Is in alien hands.
How can I unlock
To gaze at the riches
I have?

My home is loaded with gold
But run by a stranger.
I am blind
From birth.
He would let me in
Only if I pay
My door-keeping fees.

As I do not know
Who he is,
I traverse the streets
Of error. . . .

Lālan

ꕥ

Could I ever forget him
since I delivered my heart
at his feet?
His beauty enchants my eyes
round the compass
wherever I steer myself.

Though all call him black,[1]
He is not black.
He is the glow of the moon—
the black moon,
and there is no other moon to equal him. . . .

Lālan

[1] Krishna.

Sixteen gangsters[1]
of the city
are running loose,
looting all.
The five wealthy ones[2]
are nearly lost;
the trade is at the point
of breaking.

The king of kings
is also chief
of thieves.
To whom may I complain?

The riches all are gone
leaving only an empty room
to my credit.
Says Lālan:
The room will pay
for tax claims.

Lālan

I am afraid
Of the divine sport.
The boat carrying the river[3]
Marches on the land.

This is the nature
Of the Ganges of life.
Rising with the rains
It dries again
At an eyelid's wink.

[1] Five *jñānendriya*, forces of perception: ears, skin, eyes, nose and tongue for tasting; five *karmendriya*, forces action: anus, genital organ, hands, feet and tongue for speaking; and six enemies: lust, anger, greed, ignorance, pride and envy.

[2] Conscience, wisdom, restraint, renunciation and devotion.

[3] The 'boat' represents the human body and the 'river' life.

Flowers blossom
Adorning its waters,
Fruits form unseen.
And pervading all,
The fish as the preserver of life[1]
Playfully floats
In the river.

Says Lālan:
The fish too will go
When the stream evaporates.

Lālan

ꕤ

How the days drag
before my union
with the man of my heart!
Round the hours
of the day and night
as the rain-bird, *chātaka*,
watches the clouds,
I gaze at the black-moon[2]
hoping to surrender myself
at his feet—in vain.

Like lightning
flashing through the clouds
and hiding in the clouds
never to be found again,
I saw his beauty
flashing through my dream
and I lost Krishna.

Lālan

[1] The *mīn*, in the form of a fish, is the first re-incarnation of Vishnu, the preserving power of the Hindu Triple-Forces.
[2] Krishna.

The road to you is blocked
By temples and mosques.
I hear your call, my lord,
But I cannot advance—
Prophets and teachers bar my way.

Since I can wish for burning the world
With that which cools my limbs,
My devotion to unity
Is dying divided.

Doors of love bear many locks—
Scriptures and beads.
Madan, in tears,
Dies of regret and pain.

Madan

ꝏ

Even if you forbid,
Dear friend,
I am helpless.
My songs contain
My prayers.

Some flowers pray
Through the glamour of colours
And others, being dark,
With fragrance.
As the *vinā* prays
With its vibrating strings,
Do I with my songs.

Madan

ꝏ

O cruelly eager,
Are you going to fry on fire
Your heart's flower-bud?
Are you going to force it to blossom
And let the scent escape
Without biding your time?

Look at my master, God,
Eternally opening the buds to bloom
But never in a hurry.
You are dependent
On the hours of the day
Because of your terrifying greed.
What else can you do?

Listen to Madan's appeal
And do not hurt the master at heart:
The stream spontaneously flows
Lost in itself,
Listening to his words.
O my eager one.

Madan

ཋ

The subterranean stream
Flowing through the heart of the earth,
Is constantly present
And yet, invisible.

God reminds me
Of this undefined river,
And I am afraid of
Discussing him. . . .

Madan

ཋ

I shall not open my eyes again
If I do not see him at first sight.
Can you then tell me
Through the sense of smelling,
And through my listening ears:
That he has come,
That he has come
To the sky in the east—
That your friend has come
To the sky of the east.

Did the lotus bloom open its eyes
And I did not see?
But the crimson glow of the rising sun
Rocked it to sleep
On the mattress of night.
I shall not open my eyes again
If I do not see him at first sight.

Madan

ꕥ

The so-called lovers
Rarely know
The flavours of loving.
A lover lives
For love alone
As the fish in the water. . . .

Great is the lover
Who can love day and night,
and is wholly devoted
To love's intercourse—
Worship with prayers.

The man or the woman
Is still alone,
But a lover is formed
When the souls conjoin. . . .

Manohar

ꕥ

. . . Your heart
is a piece of paper
and the figures
you have written on it
cannot be known
except by the heart. . . .

Narahari

The act of loving
Is not an idle dream—
Loving grows
From the grilling of lust,
Like feeling death
Being wholly alive.

The clay-beetle
Buried in the earth
Lives on clay,
Nestling in it.

Lovers know how
Love can overcome lust—
Though an uphill walk
Even for a man of strength. . . .

Nārān

Groping for the river,
O my senseless heart,
In vain do you wander
From place to place.
The ocean of your heart
Bears a priceless gem.
What good is life
If you fail to contact
The spontaneous man[1]
Who dwells in your body?
Your destiny is shamed.

Do not give up gold
For a piece of glass,
Nor leave the heaven
For a visit to hell.
What good is there
In rushing round the world?
The eternal hero lives
In your own little room. . . .

Nitāidās

[1] *Sahaja mānush*, the spontaneous man. See note p. 73.

Plunging deep into the sea
of beauty,
some can swim
and others sink.

The jewel encrusted
on the hood of a snake
enriches the man
who can tame the beast.
Those unaware of the flavours of feelings
are bitten to death.

The jewel resting
at the bottom of the sea
is gathered by the diver
to heighten his chance.
Those unable to dive to the depth
choke and die.

Lust mingles with love
like water with milk.
And a connoisseur as pure as the swan
is able to distil it.

Nitya(?) Khyapā

ꕥ

Cry for the unknown
to know another heart.
Through the remote
find intimacy.

Gathering planks
and pieces of metal,
you build a boat
to float on the sea—
but the elements
are alien to water.
The boat sails
and the boat sinks
but the tie of love
is never torn. . . .

Nitya(?) Khyapā

I wished to turn myself
into pure gold
by touching the philosopher's stone,
but I could not do it,
alas, I could not.

Copper trickled into it—
making me an alloy. . . .

Padmalochan (Podo)

ꕥ

. . . From the distance of millions of miles
the sun rays unravel the lotus bloom,
opening its petals.

But Podo is burnt to death
in the field of lotus blooms
by the fire of feelings.

Life walks away
together with the days
but with no songs for God.

Padmalochan (Podo)

ꕥ

The moon rises
at high noon,
and yet, the night is long.

The darkest
sky of the month
is alight
with the full moon.
But the hours are still dark.

The sun has died,
striking
at our heart. . . .

Padmalochan (Podo)[1]

[1] Tape-recorded in 24 Parganas, 1954.

My eyes are drowned by shadows,
The flavours of feelings,
And the lotus of my heart
Closes in its petals
On the shore of darkness.
The waves ride the waves
On the blackened Jamunā.

Floating on the water,
The flute of love
Enters my ears—
The flute of the lord of love.
And I chase the world as a Bāul would,
Away from home,
Forgetting all.
I cry as I clutch the float
On the waters of passion.
My eyes are drowned by shadows,
The flavours of feelings.

Padmalochan (*Podo*)

ঌৡ

Do you wish to visit my
inner home
and drink nectar,
my heart?

Will you not fail to enter
where lovers march
in a joyous carnival,
singing of love?

Then walk the way
with a lamp of beauty,
leaving behind
this greed, that lust,
the ways of the world
and all qualities.[1]

[1] *Sātvika*, *rājasika* and *tāmasika*.

Blames and violence,
old age and death,
dawn and dusk,
do not live there.
Only rays of colour
brilliantly shine.

The fire has made a home
with explosives there. . . .

Padmalochan (*Podo*)

ঌ

. . . Not one single branch grows on that tree but new leaves shoot forth. The tree encompasses the entire universe, reaching millions of miles. On top of it rests a flower-bud, gently blossoming, as the bees flutter around it. So varied is the colour of the flower that the world is utterly enchanted by it.

Padmalochan (*Podo*)

ঌ

Will the man of love[1]
still wish to remain
in my broken-down home?
The spirit of my dwelling
is in total disorder.

God had brought us together:
like the hard-skinned coconut
and its thirst-quenching milk.
But how did the liquid flow
through that skin,
I would not know.

Like a dung-beetle,
I was busy making a shell
for my own death. . . .

Padmalochan (*Podo*)

[1] The 'man of love' or the 'man of heart' represents the Bāul's god.

O my heart,
Come and mingle with my heart.
With two hearts
United as one,
Let us visit
The fantastic city.

Open the doors of love
To see the divine sport—
The boat is afloat
On the dry land
And the frog sings of the god.
Strange are the ways
Of the land—
Trees have no roots.
Branches loaded with
The flavours of feelings
Rest in the sky,
Flowering, fruiting.
There is no water there
Nor any earth,
But the moat
Round the fort of the king
Is overflowing
With love. . . .

Padmalochan (*Podo*)

ಐ

In vain do you worry,
my heart,
ignoring the possibilities
of your flesh and blood.

Wholly enchained
in animal intercourse,
how can you attain
the act of loving. . . ?

Plants may be sown
by the throwing of seeds,
but care is needed
for the joys of the eyes—
the rich rice field of golden corns.

Padmalochan (*Podo*)

ꕥ

That secret of feeling,
my heart,
is in knowing it.
The riches wrapped
in a heap of rubbish
need singling out.
Sugar also glitters
when mingled with sand. . . .

Padmalochan (*Podo*)[1]

ꕥ

What makes you think
You are human?
Having squandered
Your heritage of heart,
You are now lost in lust.
It is senseless to scheme
With a lock and a key
Against your fear
Of the weaknesses of life.
Your home is in shambles
While the out-house shines
Below the moon-canopy.

God is deserting your temple
As you amuse yourself
By blowing conch-shells
And ringing bells. . . .

Padmalochan (*Podo*)[2]

[1] Tape-recorded in Siuri, Birbhum. Singer: Nabanidās Bāul.
[2] Tape-recorded in Siuri, Birbhum. Singer: Nabanidās Bāul.

Brothers,
Come along,
If you wish to smoke
The hemp of love.
With mounting intoxication
Dissolve the habits
Of your settled home,
And take shelter
In the lord of faith. . . .

He who smokes
The hemp of loving,
Is wholly unaffected
By drug. . . .

Panchānan

❧

How can the rays of the sun
conjugate with the lotus bloom?
That is love
and not to be clouded by knowledge.

Keep your soles dry
as you coast the sea.
Let attachments share the same home
but live unattached. . . .

Pāñchu

❧

Strike your master hard
And worship in faith.
If you wish to be devoted to God,
Live unattached,
Homeless, in spite of a homestead
And your life with a girl.

Do not listen to your heart
That forever misleads.
Do not only think
But chain your master hand and foot.
Cut out a cane of love
And flog him till he is blue. . . .

The master must eternally bow
At the feet of the disciple. . . .

Panchuchānd

ᘏ

The shapes you have formed
my lord,
like vessel after vessel,
tell the tale of the divine caprice
at the landing-stage of the river
and at the open field
and at the market place. . . .

Pānja Shāh

ᘏ

With a beggar's humility
I have come to your doors,
O benign bearer of pains.
No one is ever turned away
From your home of unending stores.
You have all the riches
In the worlds of god, demon and man
And so much have you given
Without my demand.
No more do I need any wealth,
O my master,
Give me your feet. . . .

Pānja Shāh

What good is there
in being proud of one's race?
What can a race do
either in this world or the other?
My heart bids me set funeral fires
to the face of the race.

All my time passes
being an honourable man,
bearing the burden of my race
and watching confusion.

People are chased away from their own lands
when the stomach pangs
and yet still they carry the load
of their stock—
the Hindus and the Mussalmans.
What is a race and what are its signs?
You cannot eat your race
nor can the race remedy an illness. . . .

Pānja Shāh

ꕥ

That astounding flower
opening on the waters of the three streams[1]
enchants the worlds.

Seen in flashes at times,
it hides below the waterline.
And with no form of its own,
the eternal bloom
is the source of joy. . . .

Pānja Shāh

ꕥ

He who has seen the beauty
of the beloved friend,[2]
can never forget it.
The form is for seeing
but not for discourse,
as beauty has no comparison.

[1] *Tribeni*, see note p. 75.

[2] God.

He who has seen that form
flashing on the mirror,
the darkness of his heart is gone.
He lives with his eyes
focussed on the form,
careless of the river between life and death.

His heart forever devoted to beauty
dares the gods. . . .

Pānja Shāh

ꕥ

He who knows the ways
of the river of life,
has no sense of fear.
Rejecting safety of the low tide,
he pulls the towing rope taut
on high tidal waves.

He bides his time by the river bank
when the tide engulfs the day.
At night when the moon ascends the sky,
he ensnares the moon.

Wide and wild is the river of life
with splendid playful waves
where three streams meet.[1]
Each of the waterways
flows true to its course
but three together is a whirlpool.

He who can seize the vortex
of the *Tribeni*,[2]
the confluence of the three streams,
can swim with the joy of love.
He is not afraid of the hazard. . . .

Phatik Chānd

[1] *Tribeni*, see note p. 75.

[2] *Ibid.*

You may hurt me, my lord
go, hurt me
as long as I can bear the pain.

Sorrow weighs down on me
and I bear it bending
in spite of my emasculated limbs. . . .

Podu

ꕥ

. . . Ants wishing to fly
Are endowed with wings
But never can turn into birds.
They lose their lives
To devouring birds.

Prasanna

ꕥ

A leper does not fret over
the ordinary fever.
His bed being the ocean
he is not afraid of the dew.

When love is still true
to the anguish of parting,
sorrows for oneself
sink in the sea of grief. . . .

Prasanna

ꕥ

The act of finding
Is not for the highest;
By being humble
You can reach life's God.

Clouds pour down
On the hollow of the earth,
But the lowest of the wells
Guards the water as a blessing. . . .

Prasanna

. . . A restless rutting elephant repels control
but the *mahout* deters the beast
by his driving hook
and leads the elephant to the battlefield.

Lust must be charged
by the arrow of love,
in the arena of passions.
The vigilant will never be vanquished. . . .

Prasanna Kumār

ꕥ

Have you tallied,
My heart,
The number of ways
Of finding him
In the city of love?
The treasure of life
Shuns bogus reckonings.

The world is a carnival
Where lovers meet
Like children of games.
Figure out
The nature of your feelings
For the jewel of your life.

He is reached in the way
Each seek to reach him:
Through tender passion
Or servitude,
Through loyalty
Or parental care.
Or through the love
Of tranquility, peace. . . .

Find the feelings
Which are born with you,
And then worship him
With your own strength.

Punya

O my heart,
Imprisoned in a cave of darkness
Forever knowing nothing,
You sleep unaware,
O my feelingless heart,
And the treasure of worship
Slips away from you.
How can you go drunken
With meaningless precepts?
What good is there in roaming
From place to place?
You have never ceased to think.
Instead of shaving your heart's desires
You have shaved your head
To look like a sage.
My foolish heart,
Your passions like tigers
Are ready to leap,
And the doors of the senses
Are blocked by the mind,
How will you escape?
Purify the two poles of your being
And the master will come to your aid.

Says Rādhānāth: Who can ferry you
Across the stream of life
But God as your helmsman?
Abandon masters, my foolish heart,
And worship God.

Rādhānāth[1]

ꝏ

While desire
Burns in the limbs,
Still there is time.
Boil the juice
On the fire of longing
To condense
The fluid.

[1] Tape-recorded in Siuri, Birbhum. Singer: Purna Chandra, son of Nabanidās Bāul.

The sweetness of sirop
Will ferment and sour
Unless it is stirred
On controlled heat.
Feelings evolve from desire
And love shoots forth
From lust. . . .

Rādhāshyām

ꙮ

Explore the nature
Of your own body,
My unfeeling heart!
Unless you know
Your very substance,
Worshipping God
Is of no avail.
The body is the home
Of seven heavens,
The nether-world
And the earth we live in,
For you to voyage. . . .
You will blunder
My unseeing heart,
As you never learnt to know
The friends and the foes
Alive in your body. . . .

Rādhāshyām

ꙮ

The man is living in man[1]
Wholly intermingled.
O my unseeing heart,
Your eyes are unwise.
How then can you
Locate the treasured man?
The unseen man
Dwelling in the brilliance of light
Hides his identity
From those blinded by stupor.

[1] *Mānush*, meaning the man, in Bāul terms refers to God.

He is stationed in man,
Appearing and vanishing
As the eyelids blink. . . .

Rādhāshyām

ꩮ

Now is the time for you
to repeat the names
of Rādha and Krishna—
the gods of devoted love.

The central beam
of your life is down,
and the time is gone.
Your cheeks are sunk
and your hair is sagging
dead as a mop of jute.
Now is the time to repeat
Rādhā and Krishna's names.

A fading rainbow,
you balance on a stick,
and crouch as a letter of the alphabet—
with your knees and head together.
Your time has gone away
and all for nothing.
Your teeth are missing,
but your eyes, as empty holes,
still frown from your brows.

Rāmachandra

ꩮ

. . . My heart is eager enough
but shy at work.
It knows but never learns.
And as fast as an eyelid blinks,
it creates catastrophes
and drives me away from place to place.

My heart is like a horse
with five pairs of reins round its neck[1]
and is pulled in five directions all at once,
by five pairs of hands. . . .

Rām Gosāiñ

ᘐᘏ

My plaited hair
is still intact
and dry
though I stand in the stream
and splash
and swim about the river.
I cannot be touched by water.

I tend to all the household work—
cooking, arranging
and offering food—
but I am not touched
by the kitchen or the home.

I am neither loyal
nor disloyal,
but I cannot abandon my lord of love.

Rasarāj Goswāmi[2]

ᘐᘏ

My heart,
Dress yourself
In the spirit of all women[3]
And reverse
Your nature
And habits. . . .[4]

[1] The five elements—earth, water, fire, air and ether.
[2] Tape-recorded in Siuri, Birbhum. Singer: Nabanidās Bāul.
[3] *Prakriti*, feminine energy.
[4] In order to achieve consciousness, the Bāul considers that it is sometimes necessary to adopt the opposite nature to one's own so as to be able to unite the male and the female elements in oneself.

Millions of suns
Will burst open
With brilliance,
And the formless
In visual forms.
You will see
What cannot be seen
Only if you can be
The formless
In you. . . .

Rupchānd

ꕥ

A creature of lust
Is easily seen
As he is full of signs.
Like the ant
Learning to fly,
He is unafraid of death.
Like a vulture
That soars high above
Only to swoop
At the garbage heap,
A man of lust
Falls for a bag of sex,
Forgetting his vows.

Love never can be
In lust alone,
Tāran,
Worship your master.

Tāran

ꕥ

NOTES ON THE POETS

Ananta Gosāiñ: Well known among the West Bengal Bāuls, Ananta comes from Balshigram of Bankura district. He is known to have died toward the close of the nineteenth century.

Bishā Bhuñimālī: The song translated in this volume comes from the collection of Shri Kshitimohan Sen Shastri. According to the collector, Bishā was a disciple of Balarām Bāul who belonged to the Hindu Kaivarta caste.

Chandidās Gosāiñ: Chandidās Gosāiñ died in 1938. There were many improbable stories told about him, such as that he lived 151 years. He made his home in Nabadwip but originally came from the Namahshudra caste from the village Kamarhati in the district of Jessore. He left several disciples.

Erfān Shāh: Well-known Bāul from Barasat of twenty four Parganas, Erfān Shāh has left a number of disciples. Dates of birth and death are uncertain.

Gangārām: Gangārām belonged to the Namahshudra caste and, though older, was a great friend of Madan Bāul, also presented in this volume. The two songs translated here come from Shri Kshitimohan Sen Shastri's collection. According to Shri Sen Shastri's assessment, the teacher of Gangārām was Mādhā.

No precise date is available, but Gangārām is known to have been a great Bāul.

Gosāiñ Gopāl (*Rāmgopāl Joyārdār*)*:* Born in 1869, in village Shilaidaha Kushtia, Rāmgopāl came from a Vaishnava Brāhman family. His father was Rāmlāl Joyārdār, his mother Manomohini. Guru: his father Rāmlāl.

Rāmgopāl learned to read and write at an early age but he was mainly interested in singing. He followed the Vaishnava faith as a Bāul, and had a large number of disciples among both the Hindu and the Muslim communities. He was well known for his great healing power. He changed his name into Gosāiñ Gopāl when he became a Bāul. Died 1912.

Hāude Gosāiñ: Born in Medtalā, Bardhaman in 1795, of a Brāhman family. His family name before he became a Bāul was Matilāl Sānyāl. His father was Haladhar Sānyāl, his mother Shyāmāsundari.

Well educated in Sanskrit literature and Hindu theology, Matilāl adopted the name of Hāude Gosāiñ when he became a Bāul. He had two teachers: Bashishthānanda Swāmi, who taught the Tantrik texts, and Prahlādānanda Goswāmi, who was his teacher in Vaishnava theology before Matilāl became a Bāul and adopted the name Hāude.

Ishān Jugi: Ishān belonged to the Hindu Jugi caste, possibly related to the Nāth sect. He was the teacher of Madan Bāul who came from an Islamic family. The songs of Ishān translated for this volume are from Shri Kshitimohan Sen Shastri's collection.

Jādubindu: Jādubindu came from village Panchloki of the district of Bardhaman. The dates of his birth and death are uncertain. His teacher was a Bāul named Kubir.

Jādubindu has left quite a large number of songs, probably a couple of hundred. A true Bāul, of peasant origin, Jādubindu uses the simple imagery of village life. The fisherman, the ploughman, the boatman and the tools of their respective trades are the subjects of Jādubindu's poetry. As a result, his songs are extremely popular with the peasant communities of Bengal.

Kālāchānd: Kālāchānd was a carpenter by profession and possibly belonged to the Namahshudra caste. The teacher of Kālāchānd was Nityanāth.

Lālan: Born in the village Bhandra, at that time in the district of Nadia, but now in Kustia. Age uncertain, but it is estimated that he was born in 1775 and died in 1891.[1]

Lālan came from a Hindu Kāyastha family, with the family name of Kar or Das. From childhood, he is known to have been religious. According to the popular belief Lālan married young. During a walking pilgrimage to Puri, to the famous Hindu temple of Jagannath, he had a severe attack of smallpox and was abandoned by his travel companions who feared contamination. A Muslim Bāul family took pity on him and kept him in their home, where he recovered and lived as a member of the family. He then became a Bāul and married his second wife, a Muslim girl.

Lālan's songs are as popular among the Bāuls of West Bengal as in the East, largely because of his use of both Muslim and Hindu imagery and thought. Many of his songs were tape-recorded by the translator during his journey in West Bengal.

Madan: The majority of Madan Bāul's songs translated in this volume come from Shri Kshitimohan Sen Shastri's collection. According to Shri Sen Shastri, Madan was born a Mussulman. His teacher was Ishān Jugi, belonging to the Hindu Jugi caste.

A close friend of Madan was the Bāul Gangārām, also presented in this book. Shri Sen Shastri, in his book *Bānglār Bāul*, is cautious

[1] *Bānglār Bāul O Bāul Gān*, Upendranath Bhattacharya, Calcutta, 1957.

about dating Madan, but judging from the language these songs could not have been written earlier than the end of the nineteenth century.

Padmalochan (*Podo*): Very little information about Padmalochan's life is available. It is commonly believed by the Bāuls of today that he came from the Rārh districts of Bengal and was one of the early Bāuls, whose songs have been passed orally from teacher to disciple. It is believed that Padmalochan may have lived toward the end of the eighteenth century.

Pānja Shāh: Born in the district of Jessore in 1851, Pānja Shāh died in 1914. Highly respected by the Bāuls of both Hindu and Muslim communities, his songs are popular in different districts of Bengal, East and West.

Phatik Chānd: Born in Faridpur, in a Hindu Namahshudra family, Phatik Chānd lived a long time in Nabadwip, the centre of the Bengali Vaishnava movement. He died toward the middle of this century.

Rādhāshyām: The original home of Rādhāshyām was the village Indas in the district Bankura but he lived mostly in Chandpur, Birbhum, in the ashram of his teacher Guruchand Goswāmi. His dates are uncertain.

BIBLIOGRAPHY

Bengali

Bandopadhyay, Somendranath, *Bānglār Bāul—Kāvya O Darshan*, Calcutta, 1964.

Bhattacharya, Asutosh, (ed.) *Bangiya Loka-Sangit Ratnākara*, Vol. I, Calcutta, 1966.

Bhattacharya, Upendranath, *Bānglar Bāul O Bāul Gān*, Calcutta, 1957.

Chattopadhyay, Pashupati, (ed.) *Bāul Sangit*, Calcutta, 1964.

Das, Matilal & Mahapatra, Piyushkanti, (ed.) *Lālan Gitika*, Calcutta, 1958.

Das, Tarachand, (ed.) *Bāul Sangit*, Calcutta, 1961.

Deva, Chittaranjan, *Banglār Palligīti*, Calcutta, 1966.

Devi, Indira, *Bānglār Sādhak Bāul*, Calcutta, 1962.

Rāy, Kalidas, *Padāvali Sāhitya*, Calcutta, 1961.

Prāchin Banga Sāhitya, Vol. I, Calcutta, no date.

Rāy, Sitanath, (ed.) *Brihat Bāul Sangit*, Calcutta, no date.

Sen Shastri, Kshitimohan, *Bānglar Bāul*, Calcutta, 1954.

Bānglar Sādhanā, Calcutta, 1965.

Hindu-Musalmāner Jukta Sādhanā, Calcutta, 1949.

Shil, Nandalal, (ed.) *Bāul Sangit*, Calcutta, no date.

English

Archer, W. G., *The Loves of Krishna*, London, 1957.

Basham, A. L., *The Wonder that was India*, London, 1954.

Bhattacharya, Deben, (transl.) *Love Songs of Vidyāpati*. ed. W. G. Archer, London, 1963.

Love Songs of Chandidās, London, 1967.

Mookerjee, Ajit, *Tantra Art*, Paris—New York—New Delhi, 1966.

Sen, Dinesh Chandra, *History of Bengali Language and Literature*, Calcutta, 1911.

DISCOGRAPHY

BAM LD 099:	*Religious Songs from Bengal*— Songs of the Bāuls and Poems of Chandidās, La Boite a Musique, Paris.
BAM LD 015:	Musique Religieuse de l'Inde, La Boite a Musique, Paris.
V.41:	Rythmes et Melodies du Bengale, Club Francais du Disque, Paris.
427 016 NE:	Songs from Bengal, Philips, Baarn, Holland.
SPL 1614:	Folk Music of Northern India, Period Records, New York.
ECLP 2256:	Folk Songs of Bengal, H.M.V., Dum Dum, India.

INDEX

Abbass-uddin, 50n
Adhar-chand, 84n, 89n
Adhar Mānush, 37, 64n, 73n
Aektārā (string drone), 28, 29
Allahabad, 75n
Ānandalahari (or *gubgubi*, or *khamak*), plucking drum, 28

Bānglār Bāul, 35n
Bengal, 23–26
Bengali Poetry, 27
Bhatktadas Bāul, 83n
Bhattacharya, Deben, 27n, 73n
Bhuñimālī, Bisha, 27–28, 53
Bijamantra ('seed-words'), 47n, 62n
Bindu, 78n
Birajā, river, 73n
Birbhum, 47n, 76n, 102n, 109n, 112n
Brahmā, 51n
Bratakatha, poems, 23
Brindāban, 69n
Buddhists, 25, 26

Campbell, Roy, 34n
Chaitanya Deva, Shri, 27n, 33, 37
Chānd, Phatik, 106
Chandidās, 27n
Chandra (moon), 45n
Chandra, Purna, 47n, 76n, 109n
Charan, Gosāiñ, 63
Chātaka, 81n
Chiru, 57
Choudda poyā, 52n

Dās, Gobinda, 60
Dās, Gobne, 61
Debnath, Haripada, 51n
Dhāmāli, 27
Dīn, 57
Dol (spring festival), 31
Dotārā (lute), 28–29
Duggi (kettle drum), 29
Dvidal, 88n

Festivities in Bengal, 24, 31
Fikirchānd, 58

Gājam, dances
Gambhirā, dances
Gangārām, 59
Ganges, river, 75n
Gopāl, 24n, 61, 62
Gopāl, Gosāiñ, 32n, 36n, 63, 64, 65, 66
Gopijantra (or *aektārā*), string drone, 28, 29
Gosāiñ, Chandidās, 33n, 54, 55, 56
Gosāiñ, Hāude, 31n, 32n, 33n, 68–71
Gosāiñ, Ram, 112
Goswāmi, Rosarāj, 112
Gubgubi (plucking drum), 28
Guruchānd, 66

Haridās, 67, 68
Hierococcyx varius, 81n
Himalayas, 24
Hindu
  kings in Bengal, 26
  faith in Bengal, 30
Hindu Triple-Forces, Power of the, 51n, 92n

Ibid, 106n
Idā, vessel, 52n
Ishān, Jugi, 34n, 71n, 72, 73
Islam, 26, 30

Jādubindu, 73–76
Jain, 25
Jamuna, river, 75n
Jhāpān, songs, 23
Jñanendriya (forces of perception), 91n
Juri (bell-metal cymbals), 29

Kachan-janghā peaks, 23
Kailāshchandra, Dwija, 24n, 57
Kālāchānd, 25n, 77, 78
Kānāi, 79, 85n
Kānāilāl, 79
Karam, songs, 23
Karma, 84n
Karmendriya (forces of action), 91n
Kāshi, 84n
Khamak (plucking drum), 28
Khyapā, Nitya (?), 97
Krishna, 27n, 45n, 58n, 61n, 69n, 73n, 89n, 90n, 92n
Krishnadās, 79

Kshitimohan Sen Shastri, 35n
Kumār, Prasanna, 108

Lālan, 37n, 80–92
Love Songs of Chandidās, 27n, 73n

Madan, 37n, 93–95
Madhurya, 83n
Manmatha, god, 69n
Manohar, 95
Mānush, 110n
Mantra, 47n
Mathnawi (Rumi, Jalalu'l-Din), 34
Mīn, 63n, 64n, 92n
Mon, 83n
Mukerjee, Ajit, 32n
Mūladhāra-chakra, 70n
Muslims in Bengal, 26

Nabanidās Bāul, 29–30, 47n, 76n, 102n, 109n, 112n
Narahari, 95
Nārān, 96
Nitāidās, 96

Padmalochan (Podo), 30n, 37n, 98, 102
Pāla kings, ruling in Bengal, 26
Pānchāli, poems, 23
Panchānan, 103
Pāñchu, 103
Panchuchānd, 104
Pingalā, vessel, 52n
Podu, 35n, 107
Prakriti, 112n
Prasanna, 107
Prayag, 75n
Punya, 108

Rādhā, 27n, 73n, 89n
Rādhānāth, 109
Rādhāshyām, 110, 111
Rājasika, 99n
Rāmachandra, 111
Ramakrishna Bāul Sangha, 43n, 44n
Rasik, 89n
Religious Songs from Bengal, 83n

Rig Veda, 34, 35
Rumi—poet and mystic, 34n
Rumi, Jalalu'l-Din, poet, 34
Rupchānd, 113

Sahaja, 73n
Sahaja mānush, 96n
St John of the Cross, 34
Sanskrit, 47n
  influence of Bengal, 25–26
Saptalok, 52n
Saptapātāl, 52n
Saraswati, river, 77n
Saturn, *see* Shani
Satvika, 99n
'Seed-words' (*Bījamantra*), 47n
Sena kings in Bengal, 26
Shāh, Erfān, 57, 58
Shāh, Pānja, 104–106
Shani, the Saturn (astral god), 23, 25
Shashthi, goddess, 23
Shiva, 51n
Shri Chaitanya Deva, 27n, 33, 37
Shushumnā, vessel, 52n
Siuri, 47n, 76n, 102n, 109n, 112n
'Songs of the Soul in Rapture' (St John), 34
Sūfīs, 26, 34

Tāmasika, 99n
Tantra Art, 32n
Tantras, 32, 33, 36
Tāj Mahla, 31
Tāran, 113
Tribeni, 63n, 75n, 105n, 106n

Vaishnava Hindus in Bengal, 26
Vaishnava, poetry, 33
  metric structure of, 27
Varanasi, 51n, 84n, 85n
Vedas, 32, 35, 37
Vedic Hindu, 25
Vedic poetry, 35
Vishnu, 92n
Vushuddha-chakra, 69n

Yoga, 66n